KILLERS

KEEP

SECRETS

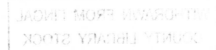

James Huddle
848 N Rainbow Blvd 4296
Las Vegas NV 89107

ISBN: 978-1-7339732-0-5 (print)
ISBN: 978-1-7339732-1-2 (ebook)

Ordering Information:
Special discounts are available on quantity purchases by corporations, associations, and others. For details, contact jimhuddle@yahoo.com

KILLERS KEEP SECRETS

THE
GOLDEN STATE KILLER'S
OTHER LIFE

JAMES HUDDLE

CONTENTS

CHAPTER 1

"DO YOU KNOW JOSEPH JAMES DEANGELO?"

I had stopped by my daughter's house to visit on April 25, 2018, when I got the phone call. The caller ID said New York, but I wasn't expecting a call from the other side of the country. Curious, I answered and put the phone on speaker.

The caller identified himself as Jason Silverstein, a reporter with *Oxygen*.

"Is this James Huddle?" Silverstein asked.

"Yes," I answered.

"Do you know Joseph James DeAngelo?"

"Yes."

Joe had been like a brother to me for decades, even after he and my sister, Sharon, separated. My kids grew up near his kids. Of course, I knew him.

"Did you know he was arrested for being the Golden State Killer?"

"Killer?" I said. *What the hell?*

Silverstein asked if I knew about the East Area Rapist.

I told him I remembered. I'd lived in Orangevale, a part of the East Area of Sacramento, California, during the 1970s when the attacks were happening. The East Area Rapist was a big deal. People were scared into locking their doors at night. Joe had been connected to those crimes, too, Silverstein told me.

My mind was racing at this point. I remembered Joe asking me about the East Area Rapist once. He asked me what I would do if the East Area Rapist came into my house. "I'd attack the guy," I told Joe. "He only has a knife and I may harm him so that he may be caught." Joe never brought it up again.

As the reporter began to ask more questions, I told him I needed time.

"Oh, my goodness," I said. "Wow. I'll have to process this."[1]

When I hung up the phone, I looked at my daughter, Deanna, who'd been listening. Her eyes, like mine, were as big as saucers.

For a couple minutes, it felt like it could have all been a mistake, some misunderstanding. But then my other daughter, Nicole, called. She was crying. She'd seen her uncle Joe's house on the news, cordoned off by crime tape. Her cousin, Misha, still lived there at the time.

That day, I learned that authorities believed my former roommate, longtime friend, and brother-in-law was responsible for killing more than a dozen people and raping at least 50 across California between 1975 and 1986. Using DNA evidence, the FBI connected him to the crimes, though it's important to note at the time of this writing that Joe hasn't entered a plea. The brutal attacker had been known by various nicknames through the years: the Golden State Killer, the East Area Rapist, the Visalia Ransacker, the Diamond Knot Killer, and the Original Night Stalker. Though the trial has not yet taken place, and he is innocent until proven guilty in a court of law, law enforcement is confident he's responsible. If he's convicted, prosecutors plan to ask for the death penalty.

It seems he stopped committing crimes after 1986. People wondered then what had happened. Was the Golden State Killer dead? Had he been arrested? Decades later, people still wondered what had happened to stop such a prolific serial killer.

I didn't know then what kind of monster he really was. In 1981, I celebrated as Joe and Sharon had their first baby girl, born about a month apart from my second daughter, Nicole. Five years after that, they had their second, and two and a half years later they had their third.

For the most part, Joe seemed like a normal guy. If he'd flaunted his crimes or paraded around celebrating the horrific things he'd done, I would have turned him in—same goes for my other relatives. If he'd been obvious about it, it wouldn't have taken law enforcement more than 40 years to catch him. Joe was hiding in plain sight.

When reporters first started calling me, I was still in a

defensive mode. I'd tell them he was innocent until proven guilty. After a couple of weeks of calls, I told them to call me again in a year, then I stopped answering my phone.

Frankly, it was all hard for me to believe at first. It's been almost two years now since the news broke. I've had time to process it, and I think it checks out.

Looking back, I remember some strange things about Joe. But none of those things would have been grounds for me to call the police. I hope that by writing this book, I can offer up what I did know about him. Maybe it will help someone else stop a bad guy a little sooner. Maybe the publicity will piss off Joe enough to say something more to the police about the crimes.

Most of Joe's immediate family don't want to have anything to do with this book, including my sister Sharon. This is a difficult time for them, and I want to respect their wishes as much as possible.

Everything I write here is to the best of my recollection, which I'll admit isn't what it used to be as I get closer to turning 70.

But I need to write this book for me. It will help me sleep at night. There's nothing anyone can do to bring back the killer's victims or restore the lives that were shattered, but I hope in some small way I can do my part to help justice prevail.

CHAPTER 2

MY SISTER'S CHARMING NEW BOYFRIEND

I first met Joe around the summer of 1971, when Sharon brought him over to meet the family. They'd recently started dating; she was 17 at the time. I was 20. I had my own place then, but I often ate dinner at Mom and Dad's house. We had just finished dinner when the doorbell rang. When Mom answered it, Sharon came in with a huge smile, followed by her new friend.

This is Joe! she said. I want you to meet Joe.

He was a bit apprehensive, as many guys are when they meet their girlfriend's family, but we got to talking. He was studying criminology to be a police officer. Sharon had just started going to American River College in northern Sacramento and planned to be a lawyer. She must have thought he was perfect.

I learned he was a Navy guy who had served for 22 months, shipping off to Vietnam. He had served on a guided missile cruiser called the *USS Canberra*, which patrolled along the 17th parallel, a circle of latitude marking the split between warring North and South Vietnam. He was injured when his ship traveled south to battle in the Mekong Delta. He served as a damage-control man then. Once, he had to repair damage to the ship when it took fire. In the effort, he lost the tip of the index finger on his right hand. It was a minor defect—the longer I knew him, the less I noticed it. But nonetheless, it was a distinguishing mark—one that could have prompted a rapist or killer to wear gloves during every attack to protect his identity.

Joe was born in Bath, New York. His father's name was Joseph DeAngelo, Senior, and his mother's name was Kathleen DeGroat. The two got married in 1941 in a Baptist church. They had Joe in November of 1945.[2]

Joseph Sr. served as an airman in World War II. According to a 1944 article in the *Elmira Star-Gazette*, he was awarded seven clusters to the Air Medal for meritorious achievement. He was wounded in action over Australia. At the time, he was serving with the Army Air Force as a gunner on a B-24 bomber.[3]

Joseph Sr. and Kathleen eventually split, and Kathleen remarried Jack Bosanko, who served in the Navy in World War II. Kathleen and Jack moved with Joe and his siblings to Auburn, California, when Joe was a teenager. Joseph Sr., who also served during the Korean War, died in South Korea in 1995. Kathleen died in 2010.

When Joe finished with his Navy service, he applied the skills he learned there and elsewhere to all kinds of mechanical and fix-it work, diving into an array of handyman projects. His stepdad, Jack, helped him get a job at Sierra Crane and Hoist in Auburn. He worked there while he studied for his associate degree.

I was in the Navy Reserve when I met Joe. The war was in full swing, and thousands of soldiers were returning in caskets. I fulfilled my military duty without having to go to Vietnam. Nevertheless, it was nice to find some common ground with Joe right off the bat.

At some point during the conversation, Joe mentioned he was looking for a place to live. I think he was living in Rancho Cordova, California, with a family member at the time.

I'm an easygoing guy. At times, I can be a little too open and friendly. I'd just met the guy, but I was already telling him my roommate Steve might have a room open in Citrus Heights, California.

The whole conversation that night lasted maybe half an hour, but by the end of it I had told him I'd ask Steve about Joe moving in. Steve owned the house, so ultimately it was his call.

Joe ended up moving in, but he didn't stay long—Steve kicked him out not long after. I was never sure why; Steve was a little weird. When Joe moved his stuff out, he told me I'd be next. He was right—I was kicked out about a month later for smoking. Steve had apparently found a cigarette butt.

After I got evicted, I called Joe.

"Oh, I knew that was going to happen," Joe said. "I have room for you. It's a two-bedroom."

Joe said he thought Steve's new girlfriend was the one who wanted us gone, and whatever she wanted from Steve, she was bound to get. Today I wonder: Did she catch Joe doing something inappropriate?

I asked him about rent, and he said it was something I could easily afford. I was happy to have a place to stay. I had liked living with him before, so I moved in.

During that time, we didn't get in each other's way. We both worked a lot and spent time with our girlfriends. We each did our own thing. He was neat and tidy—you get that way from being in the Navy.

I remember he'd take out a bottle of jalapeno chilies and munch on them like they were dill pickles. I thought it was gross. I never did like spicy things, but as far as roommate differences go, that was pretty mild.

Joe had gone to Sierra College in Rocklin before switching to Sacramento State. I later learned he'd been engaged to a woman he met at Sierra College named Bonnie just before he got involved with my sister. The two had announced their engagement May 1970 in the *Auburn Journal*.

Joe took Bonnie on harrowing motorcycle rides, and once even broke a dog's neck when it snapped at the bike, she told the *Los Angeles Times*. He took her hunting, and she suspected he had killed a number of animals illegally.[4]

Bonnie broke it off with him after he asked her to cheat for him so he would pass his Abnormal Psychology class, according to the *Times*. He tried to force her at gunpoint to run away with him to get married in Reno, but her father talked Joe down.

Within the year, Joe started dating Sharon.

We didn't know then about the darker details of his previous relationship, though he did tell me once when we were roommates that Bonnie was the love of his life. It didn't bother me much; he'd said some other strange things, too. I just thought that's how he was.

"I got your sister last night," he bragged once.

"Hey, you are talking about my sister?" I replied instantly.

It wasn't enough to make me stop being friends with him, but I did think it was weird. That's just not something you say to your girlfriend's brother.

But Sharon seemed so happy with Joe, I didn't see a need to tell her about those little things.

I took Joe flying for the first time in 1971, according to my logbook. We went up in the Aeronca Champ I flew to get flight hours under my belt. It was a small, two-person plane with a 90HP engine and high wings. The plane was designed for sport flying and people like me looking to earn their wings in the sky.

I had gotten my student pilot's license and started flying when I was 16—before I had even gotten my driver's license. My dad drove me to the airport for flight lessons, and I worked for a man across the street who had his own janitorial service to save up and pay for my lessons. I cleaned church pews, dusted off seats, and cleaned toilets. Sometimes he would wax floors and I'd buff them. I got my pilot's license when I was 17 and my multi-engine license while I was stationed at the Naval Air Station in Tennessee. The local Aero Club had a twin Piper for rent. It was only $15 per hour, which was an incredible deal then.

I loved seeing the ground below and the sky above. I loved being up in the air with the birds. I'd always hoped to work as a commercial pilot, but I had bad timing. I was competing for pilot jobs against all the Air Force guys who had college degrees after Vietnam. Even though I didn't fly professionally, I always loved it. I earned a commercial license and an instrument rating.

The first time I took Joe up, he seemed apprehensive about it. But he eventually got used to it and enjoyed the ride. We flew several times together, sometimes just flying around town for fun. We felt so free seeing houses turn into miniature homes, lining the winding, snaking roads below. Up in the sky, we didn't worry about all the obligations we left on the earth below.

We went dirt biking often, too. Joe was particularly fond

of one hill he called the Widow Maker. It was a tall, imposing hill, maybe 40 feet or so, that got incredibly steep toward the end. I had to lean forward into it, holding my breath and begging the universe to make it possible. It was challenging, but even when we fell and tumbled across the dirt, we had a good time. And we'd fall off the bike just about every third or fourth time we rode the damn hill. It got our hearts pumping like mad, and we thought it was worth the scrapes and bruises. Even so, I believe Joe was more of a thrill-seeker and risk-taker than I was.

CHAPTER 3

THE BROTHER (I WISH) I NEVER HAD

In 1972 and 1973, reports started to crop up about a cat burglar around Rancho Cordova. According to police documents, cat burglary is a rare thing, and it's often linked to sexual offenses. While Joe hasn't been charged with those crimes, law enforcement suspects this was how it all started.

Experts widely agree serial killers don't typically get their start by killing people right away. They often commit lesser crimes beforehand, gradually becoming more violent. Maybe they start by killing animals, shoplifting, or peeping in on women.

According to police documents, the Cordova Cat Burglar struck more than 30 times between 1972 and 1973. There was a gap at the end of 1972, but police noted the activities picked up again by spring of 1973.[5]

The burglar entered homes quietly after the residents were asleep. He'd leave the home using a different pre-opened door. According to police, the burglar would often strike the area between Dolecetto Drive and Malaga Way near Coloma Road, not too far from Lincoln Highway. He'd also strike in Rancho Cordova, Carmichael, Citrus Heights, and other nearby areas. The Cordova Cat Burglar was known to take purses and wallets. Sometimes he'd take car magnets and pictures.

During this time, some women reported that they had seen a man without pants standing at their windows. Sometimes this mysterious man, who police now believe could have been Joe, would sneak into homes at night, touch women who were sleeping, and run off when they woke up.

Once, a woman woke up to the burglar touching her breasts, according to police documents. She told him he needed to leave, and he did. She was alone in the house during the incident.

Another woman reported she woke up when she heard a strange sound in her bedroom. She saw a man standing near the bedroom door, about eight feet away. She sat up, and the man pointed a gun at her. The woman didn't say anything after she saw the gun, but the burglar did.

"I just took a dollar off your dresser," he said.

The woman told him to put the dollar back and leave. The burglar did leave—and he put two dollars back on the dresser, despite claiming he only took the one bill.

The man walked down the hallway, stopping to look at the woman's 17-year-old daughter, according to police documents. Before he left, he took a quarter and a nickel from a table near the door.

The burglar was also known to kill dogs. Pups, a 10-year-old dog in Rancho Cordova, was one of the early victims. The local paper, the *Grapevine*, reported the death in 1972.[6]

Three of the Citrus Heights cat burglaries were within a block of one of the two East Area Rapist strikes four years later, according to police documents. The Rancho Cordova strikes were within blocks or closer to the Rancho Cordova East Area Rapist attacks. If it's true that Joe was the Cordova Cat Burglar, he committed some of those crimes while he lived with me.

When I was younger, I was a very sound sleeper. Once my head hit the pillow around 11 p.m., I was usually out until about 6 a.m. Nothing short of an air horn could have roused me. I can't help but rack my brain now for any clue or sign he was up to no good. But I wasn't keeping close tabs on him then. I was just trying to be a good roommate and a friend.

At 69, I'm a much lighter sleeper now, and thoughts of Joe and what he's done kept me up at night.

Joe finished out his bachelor's degree in criminal justice in 1972, soon before the crimes seemed to begin.[7] Most police officers didn't have college degrees back then, let alone degrees in criminal justice. Most still don't. According to the National Police Foundation, about 30% of police officers in the US in 2019 had four-year degrees. Joe's military training and college education gave him an edge over officers with less training.

A portrait of Joe as a mastermind criminal has emerged since his arrest. I just don't know if I can believe it. I never would have called Joe quick-thinking or particularly bright. He took his time to mull things over and wrap his mind around various concepts. He was focused and thorough in planning his model-building so the result was near perfection, but he was no genius.

When I learned he tried to cheat off Bonnie to avoid failing a class, it made sense to me. I couldn't help but wonder then if he had help getting through school.

But it would be several decades before I learned about that side of Joe. At this point, we were just typical guys who did common interest things together. We didn't hang out or drink beer together. I was surprised that he drank beer. I learned that after reading crime reports.

Joe got a bit competitive with me over the dirt bikes. When I upgraded mine, he'd be sure to get one that was a little bigger. He was enchanted by mechanical things that displayed power, like guns, motorcycles, cars, and full-sized boats—a common thing for the men in my generation.

We were both young and the thrill of it all appealed to us. We could fly down the highway, wind whipping at our faces and tugging at our clothes, and nothing else mattered. It was the perfect way to beat back the drudgery of punching the clock just to get paid.

The "keeping up with the Joneses" bit started when

I bought a Honda CB350. It was a twin-cylinder, four-stroke bike known for its reliability. It served me well until I upgraded a couple years later.

Soon Joe upped the ante, buying a CB450. It was a slightly bigger bike, with a pretty green fuel tank. When I went down to Exeter, California, for a visit, Joe showed me a little Honda 125 bike he had bought. He said it was for Sharon, but I doubt she ever learned to ride. Then he showed me his new bike—a beautiful Yamaha 650—so he must have upgraded the 450.

They had moved there when Joe got hired on to work for the Exeter Police Department. He wanted to show me what his new Yamaha 650 could do, so I hopped on the little Honda 125 and went for a short ride with him. The Yamaha had some serious power behind it. I could only keep up on the Honda because Joe held back for me. Joe liked the Honda for how quiet and agile it was to ride.

I was surprised because I had bought a Honda CB750 shortly before. He stuck with the 650 for a while. Tinkerer that he was, he figured a bike with two carburetors for its two cylinders would be easier to keep tuned up. But he couldn't hold out for long. He couldn't stand the fact that my bike was bigger and faster than his.

He caved and bought a Honda CB750 of his own. Consistent with his taste, it had a green gas tank trimmed with gold. Our two bikes were almost identical—his was just a year newer and a different color. He always wanted to have the best ride.

I gave up street riding after two close calls, one ending in a nasty spill.

After that, I decided to go back to dirt biking. I didn't want my kids to end up without a father.

I bought a 2-stroke 175, a single-cylinder dirt bike, made for dirt or street. I could conquer all kinds of terrain with it. Joe saw how much fun I had on it, and he couldn't resist. He got a 250 Yamaha Trials bike. I bought a duel sport Yamaha 250XT to ride with him.

We were even. But back then, that thought hadn't crossed my mind. I grew up with three sisters, later I learned I had a fourth half-sister, and I didn't have many friends who stuck around after high school. We had moved in the middle of my junior year, so Joe's friendship was important to me. At the time, he was like the brother I never had.

There were a handful of incidents that now, looking back, give me reason to pause. I didn't think much of them then, but now I wonder if they were a warning of things to come.

We'd been roommates for a few months when the road rage incident happened. More than 40 years later and I still remember where it happened. It shocked me so much I couldn't forget it.

It was spring. He was about to graduate college.

Joe was driving his car up Route 40/Auburn Boulevard

in Sacramento. As we drove, I felt him jerk the wheel to get into a different lane. Another vehicle was behind us; I think he gave the finger to the guys in the other car. As they got close to our car, he sped up and made a right turn into a McDonald's parking lot. He pulled into one of the spaces. I was confused. But then I noticed the other car came in behind us.

They parked about six spaces down. Joe got out of the car and headed to the trunk. I got out of my side, still not sure what exactly we were getting ourselves into, but I could see two men from the other car starting to walk our way. Joe had something in his trunk covered with a blanket or terry cloth. As he removed the fabric, I realized he had a gun in a holster. He pulled it out, turning to face the other guys with a .357 Magnum. It was chrome and it looked heavy duty. If I had to guess now, I'd say it was a Smith & Wesson with a four-inch or six-inch barrel.

"Do you guys have a problem with us?" Joe asked, holding the gun.

Their eyes widened. Without a word, they turned on their heels and headed right back to their car.

Those guys flipped right around and disappeared! I was relieved the confrontation didn't turn into something worse that day. In those days, nothing happened like it does today. Now people who stop actually do shoot each other. But even then, it didn't sit right with me.

Joe and I got back into his car and kept driving. We were

silent for a while.

"Joe, you know you could get in trouble doing that," I said.

I didn't try to make it a big deal. I didn't say anything more about it; I just left him with that statement. He knew I didn't approve of what he did, and he was quiet for the rest of the drive.

It was scary. I didn't see what happened first, but looking back, I think Joe started it. Even then, I thought it was him, but I didn't know why he'd do something like that.

He knew the laws. He could have probably gotten away with murder by claiming self-defense if those guys had continued forward. Today I still wonder what would have happened if they had pulled a gun. He might have just shot them dead on the spot.

My suspicion is that he pulled the stunt to see how I would react. Maybe he wanted to show off for me somehow. Maybe there was something he was trying to prove.

I never told Sharon about the incident. I wondered what it would accomplish by bringing it up.

Even though the incident made me uncomfortable, I brushed it off. Now I wonder if it meant something deeper on the inside for Joe.

Little red flags can add up.

CHAPTER 4

THE LURE OF THE HUNT

In the early part of 1973, after the road rage incident, Joe and I went on a hunting trip.

I'd never owned a gun until I met Joe, but he insisted I get a gun and a hunting license so we could go out together. I'd never been a hunter either, but I got the gun and the license to give it a try.

We went on an easy trip hunting jackrabbits. They're all over the fields in the summer. When we spotted the one, I kneeled to steady myself. The rabbit was about 50 or 75 yards away sitting very still. Jackrabbits know you can see them more easily if they move.

"Okay, take the shot," Joe whispered.

So, I did, and I nailed him. It was effortless—but I didn't feel good about it. It already felt like a waste of an innocent life to me.

We walked down to look at the spoils of my hunt. It was kind of a mess. Bits of rabbit were splattered in the dirt. I'd

Leabharlanna Fhine Gall

never seen anything like it before.

"Look how he's all blown apart," Joe said.

He was excited by it. I wasn't.

Now I'm the guy who has a Buddha sitting in the corner and a Buddha tattoo. It turns out, hunting wasn't for me.

Joe enjoyed the kill, but that still wasn't enough to warn me of the horrific crimes that would follow. Plenty of people like to hunt. But looking back, it was another small red flag.

In 1973, a burglar operated in the Cordova Meadows subdivision of Rancho Cordova. Many of the incidents had details in common with what law enforcement had gathered from the Cordova Cat Burglar incidents, according to police documents. The burglar stole two car magnets used to advertise businesses and pictures of women who lived in one of the houses, including a set of nude photos taken by one woman's husband. He also took single earrings.[8]

The burglar once even emptied a bottle of prescription codeine pills into the sink but took the bottle with him. He stole a couple of guns in Rancho Cordova, including a Ruger revolver.

The burglar would often come in through a kitchen or sliding-glass door, open the window in a back bedroom, placing the screen on the bed or inside, unplug the air furnace, stack women's underwear in other rooms, and ransack the kitchen. Sometimes the burglar would even leave burnt matches on the floor.[9]

The burglar hit three houses in one day in March 1973.

First, he hit a home next door to a future East Area Rapist victim, stealing a movie camera and money from a piggy bank.

Second, a woman who would later be raped by the East Area Rapist in 1976 reported a "no loss" burglary that day, according to police documents.

Third, a burglar broke into a house across the river in Carmichael near Mission Avenue and El Camino Avenue, stealing 80 two-dollar bills and silver coins, according to police documents. The place was ransacked, and a small poodle was killed.

The burglar was also suspected to be behind several odd hang-up phone calls and strange communications—something the Golden State Killer came to enjoy.

According to police, one 17-year-old girl got a suspicious unsigned letter that read, "I love you."

She later answered several hang-up phone calls before a final call produced a voice on the other end.

"I love you. This is your last night to live," said a man in a low voice.

The girl lived next door to where, five years later, a man jumped the fence to flee after killing Brian and Katie Maggiore.[10]

CHAPTER 5

JOE BECOMES FAMILY

We both got married in 1973.

I married Cindy, my now ex-wife, on September 15. I didn't have a bachelor party or anything the night before. I wasn't one to get too rowdy or reckless. Cindy wouldn't have appreciated that either. I just hung out around the new apartment getting ready for the big day, trying not to let my nerves get to me.

We got married at a church on Winding Way in Carmichael, which is about a 20-minute drive from Rancho Cordova.

Cindy wore a beautiful long-sleeved white dress and a simple veil. Her dark brown hair fell just below her shoulders. I wore a black suit and a dapper black bow tie. Joe humored me and wore a yellow bow tie as he stood nearby that day. Both he and Sharon were part of the wedding party.

The day before my wedding, there was a report of a burglary and assault in Rancho Cordova.

Around 11 a.m., a 28-year-old woman was putting her 18-month-old son down for a nap when she heard a knock at the door, according to police documents.[11]

She assumed it was a religious solicitor and didn't answer. Just before that, she had seen a man out in the backyard whom she believed was an electrical utility man. Just in case, she'd armed herself with a handgun.

She heard a noise near the back of her house where the bedrooms were. She went to check on her son and caught a man trying to break in through the master bedroom window. When he realized he'd been seen, he ducked and ran around to the other side of the house.

The woman went around the house making sure the doors and windows were locked. She called her husband to tell him what had happened. But the man wasn't done. He forced open the door between the garage and the kitchen. His force pulled the nails holding the lock away from the frame's base, according to police documents.

The woman was surprised, but she still had the handgun. With the gun raised, she told the man if he came in, she would shoot him. He seemed to leave, walking away from the door and out of the garage.

The woman called the Sacramento Sheriff's Department to report what had happened. As she waited for police to arrive, he came at her again, quickly this time. He grabbed her hands and struggled with her for the handgun. He forced the gun toward her, but she quickly pulled it up. The gun discharged over her shoulder, and the man ran out of the garage door for a final time.

The woman, who'd been recovering from a recent surgery, briefly passed out. When she came to, she wrote out a description of the man and waited for police to get there.

Police didn't find the man.

If it was indeed Joe, he would have had time to break in and make it back for the wedding rehearsal that night.

Joe, then 27, and Sharon, then 20, married a couple months later.

From 1973 to 1976, Joe worked as a police officer, eventually becoming part of the burglary unit in Exeter. He and Sharon lived in a duplex then. Sharon was studying hard to get into law school. She buried herself in her books, often studying until 2 or 3 a.m.

Joe was interviewed for an article the year he started. When discussing the importance of law and order, it reads, James DeAngelo, Jr., believed that without law and order, "there can be no government and without a democratic government there can be no freedom.... Law enforcement is his career, he says, and his job is serving the community."[12]

Exeter is a small town. Today, it has fewer than 11,000 people. Back then it had about 5,000. Joe told me the Exeter Police Department shared a radio frequency with Farmersville, another small town. He told me if there were serious situations, the two departments would back each other up—but things were usually quiet. He told me there was usually only one officer on duty after hours. Back then, he worked the swing shift.

I went down to visit them once or twice. I went on a ride-along with him once in 1974. He was excited to show me he was a cop, and he wanted to show off his patrol car. As we drove, he pointed out all the farms and orchards. He told me he had permission to go on any land he wanted, and he knew all the farmers in the area.

I didn't question him about it. I had no reason not to believe him. But now I'm thinking he was lying. I think he said some of those things to make me—and maybe himself—believe that some boundaries he crossed were okay.

We drove on for a while, and then Joe said, "Let me show you the bats."

He pulled over near the streetlights, and we watched a cluster of bats flying around eating insects. We drove around town and he showed me the corporate yard and where the city kept the maintenance equipment. I rode with him for a couple hours.

During the ride-along, he told me that if he saw an old car that was all beat-up and the people in it were speeding, he'd give them a warning. But if he saw a brand-new Mercedes speeding, he'd give them a ticket every time. I don't know if he was telling the truth or if he said it because he wanted me to believe it. He might have said that to make himself look good. He often did that kind of thing.

Farrel Ward, an officer who worked with Joe back in Exeter, stayed at the department for about 30 years. When asked about Joe, he told the *Los Angeles Times*, "He was just overeducated for the small department of Exeter. He just knew anything you wanted to talk about.... [He had] all kinds of training. He didn't fit in with the other guys. We liked to joke and screw around and take the stress off of what we were doing. He was always serious."[13]

Joe told me once he butted heads with some folks at the police department over politics. He said sometimes officers would fudge reports to cover another officer's butt. He said they'd sometimes write things to back each other up. He said he didn't do that.

"I won't falsify reports," Joe said at one point. "If it's wrong, I'm not going to do that."

At the time he said that, it made me think he was an upstanding guy.

For all of Joe's talk about doing the right thing, the crimes with which he's been charged began when he lived in Exeter.

Dozens of homes were burglarized in Visalia, a city about 12 miles away from Exeter, between April 1974 and December 1975. It would have been an easy drive for Joe to make.

The Visalia Ransacker, as the burglar was called, didn't steal much of value. He took single earrings, wedding bands, and trading stamps. Every now and then he nabbed a hand-gun. Women came home to find their underwear scattered around, sometimes laid out on their beds. He tore up a couple of family photo albums and stole piggy banks, but he usually left cash untouched.

In 1975, the Visalia Ransacker pulled off about 120 burglaries in the area. In some cases, the Ransacker was involved in attempted sexual assaults. According to an April 2018 arrest warrant, the Visalia Police Department increased patrols in the area amid the attacks and put officers in several homes that hadn't yet been burglarized, but were within areas the Ransacker targeted, in hopes of catching the guy.[14]

Several folks who had encounters with the Ransacker saw him without any face covering during this time.

Many of the homes the Visalia Ransacker targeted were close to the College of the Sequoias, a community college off Highway 198 and S. Mooney Boulevard, which happened to be linked with drainage canals and ditches. The college is about 13 miles or so from Exeter. In the right conditions, the drive could take less than 20 minutes.

Police believe the Visalia Ransacker murdered Claude Snelling, a college journalism professor, as the Ransacker attempted to kidnap Snelling's daughter, Elizabeth. Snelling died trying to protect his daughter on Sept. 11, 1975. Elizabeth was 16 at the time. When her father chased the masked man, who broke into their home, the Ransacker—thought to be

Joe—shot him.

Police found footwear impressions under a window consistent with impressions found at several other houses that had been burglarized by the Ransacker, according to the arrest warrant. Police learned that the gun used to kill Snelling had been stolen in a previous Ransacker burglary about 11 days beforehand. More than 40 years passed before Joe was charged with Snelling's murder.[15]

CHAPTER 6

CRIMES ESCALATE WITH NO CLUES

Now with blood on his hands, the Visalia Ransacker's crimes would escalate. Yet for the man accused of the horrors, it seemed as though life was picture-perfect.

Sharon and Joe did well for themselves in the mid-1970s.

Sharon got accepted at the McGeorge School of Law in Sacramento, and Joe took a job at the Auburn Police Department.

Cindy and I lived in Orangevale then, which is about 20 miles away from Auburn. In the year before, when work slowed down, I was laid off from the Southern Pacific Railroad as a machinist helper and then as an electrician apprentice, so I started working at Terra Nova Produce.

Cindy and I had our first daughter, Deanna, in 1976. I was there when she came out; it was quite an event. Your first child is like that; you don't forget that moment. I wasn't much into diaper duty, but we adjusted well to being parents. Soon enough, Deanna was a daddy's girl.

It's also the year the East Area Rapist's crime spree began. We began hearing some news about it then. The East Area Rapist—who police now believe to be Joe—raped at least 10 people in 1976.

The East Area Rapist was known for prying open doors and windows near the back of people's homes. He typically wore a ski mask, announcing his arrival by shining a flashlight in his victims' eyes. He tied up his victims with a diamond knot—a decorative knot that has sailing and military uses—before raping the female in the homes he targeted, according to the FBI. Once he finished the sexual assault, he'd often ransack the home, taking small items such as rings, coins, and cash. When he left, he'd jump the fence and run through neighbors' backyards, avoiding roads.[16]

One of the first attacks connected to the East Area Rapist took place June 18, 1976, in Rancho Cordova. The Sacramento suburb sits about 30 miles away from Auburn, where Joe lived at the time. It's possible that it was less than a 40-minute drive.

The victim lived with her father, who was retired from the military, but he was on vacation in Florida at the time.

"I didn't hear him come in, I didn't hear anything, and all of a sudden, there was someone standing in my door," the woman told the FBI. She initially thought it might be her father, but instead she saw a menacing stranger with a knife wearing a ski mask. He bound his victim's hands and told her not to scream as he raped her.

"I just remember feeling extremely threatened," she told investigators.[17]

The attacks escalated from there.

Police say he'd plot out the attack in advance, often stalking women for days. Sometimes he'd even break in and leave tools—such as twine to tie up his victims—in the victim's home ahead of the attack.

But he didn't just target women.

On July 16, 1976, police suspect Joe was responsible for attacking a man in his garage around 5 a.m. in the Sacramento area. The victim opened his automatic garage door that morning. As he did, he heard footsteps, then saw a man wearing a dark ski mask bending down to come under the door. The unknown man came at the victim, striking him in the head and body several times, according to the arrest warrant. The victim tried to take cover under his own car, but the man in the mask pulled him back out from under the car, pulling the victim's pants down a bit in the process. The victim noticed the man wore light brown hiking boots with unusually thick soles, according to the warrant. He also noted the man wore gloves.

The victim told police he had heard footsteps near his backyard pool a few hours before the attack, but when he looked out the window, he didn't see anything. He also told police that his teenage daughter had moved out just weeks before the incident.[18]

It would have been about a 35-mile drive from Auburn.

The attacks continued that year, all about 20 or 30 miles from Joe's house—just far enough away, and in neighboring towns, ensuring that he wouldn't be considered a suspect or forced to return to the scene as a police officer to investigate.

On July 17, 1976, another rape was reported in Rancho Cordova, just a few blocks from another attack. The attack took place between 2 and 4:30 a.m.

On August 29, 1976, a woman and her two daughters were home asleep, again in Rancho Cordova. Around 3:15 a.m., the woman woke up to the sound of the wind chimes by her bedroom window clanging. She looked over at the window and saw the silhouette of a man trying to pry off her window screen, according to the arrest warrant. When she sat up, the attacker ducked down.

The woman ran to one of her daughter's rooms to wake her up, telling her someone was trying to break into the house. The two of them went to the other girl's room to wake her up, too. They looked out into the backyard to see if the man was out there but didn't see him.

The woman, daughters in tow, went to the kitchen to use the phone. As the woman dialed, they heard a curtain rod fall onto the floor. Soon, the silhouetted man stood in front of them.

"Freeze, or I'll kill you," he said.

He held a gun in one hand and a club in the other, according to the arrest warrant. The man said he just wanted money. He went to tie the woman's hands behind her back, but she fought back. The man hit her several times in the head with the club, but one of the girls was able to get out and run to the neighbor's house. The man got spooked and ran away.

When the three described the man to police, they noted he wore a black lineman-style utility belt, but no clothes from the waist down.[19]

On October 5, 1976, the East Area Rapist assaulted a woman in Citrus Heights. The woman told police she was lying in bed with her 3-year-old son when she heard someone flip on a light switch and heard unfamiliar footsteps in the hallway. The attacker proceeded to blindfold the woman and rape her.

For a while after, she could hear him walking around the house. When she no longer heard footsteps, she took the blindfold off and went to a neighbor's house for help.

Four days later, on October 9, 1976, a 19-year-old woman was raped in Rancho Cordova. Police were notified of the attack when the woman's coworker came to her house to pick her up for work.[20]

The attacker struck again at around 11 p.m. on October 18, 1976, after a woman in Rancho Cordova came home and parked her car in front of her house, as she usually did. When she went to get out of her car, a man forced his hand around her mouth. She started to fight back, but the man took out a knife and held it to her throat. He told her he wouldn't hurt her, that he only wanted her car. He tied her hands behind her back and took her around the corner, where he bound her feet, gagged her, and blindfolded her.

He told her not to move, saying he'd be back in 15 minutes. She asked him not to hurt her dog. He told her he wouldn't. Once she heard the man take off in her car, the woman managed to get free. She got into her house and called police.

The man who attacked her—police believe it was Joe— wore a heavy gray jacket that night, along with white cotton mechanic's gloves and brown desert boots.

Police found the victim's car the next day about .3 miles away from her house, and close to the scene of the October 9 attack. The woman's dog was, surprisingly, unharmed. It was locked in the trunk, barking when the car was found.

Years later, on January 4, 1978, that same woman answered a call from an unknown number. On the other end was a man who asked if she'd like him to perform oral sex on her. He told her he knew where she lived.[21]

On November 10, 1976, a 16-year-old Citrus Heights girl was home alone watching television when she heard a loud noise in the living room. Her dog began to bark and shake, according to the arrest warrant, but she wasn't too worried about it.

At some point, the attacker tied up her wrists and ankles

and took her away from her home. She was eventually able to untie herself and walk back toward her house. She went to the neighbors for help and they called police.

On December 18, 1976, a 15-year-old girl in Fair Oaks, California, stayed home with a cold while her parents went to a Christmas party. Around 7:15 p.m., she was practicing the piano when she heard strange noises in the house. She didn't think anything of it at the time. That night, the girl was raped in her home.[22]

CHAPTER 7

MASTER OF MANIPULATION

As the years passed, the attacks became more brazen, twisted, and sinister.

In 1977, the East Area Rapist became a major news story after raping at least 17 women and attempting to rape another. When the East Area Rapist targeted neighborhoods between 1976 and 1978, he'd call people only to hang up or say weird, crude sexual stuff to the person on the other line. He often called before burglaries, prowling, or sexual assaults. Police believed he used this as a tactic to learn who was home and who might be vulnerable to attack.[23]

Around this time, I remember Joe displaying some of his manipulative nature. He even brought me in on one of his schemes. It wasn't significant enough then for me to think much of it, but looking back I wonder if it was more significant.

In the mid-1970s, Joe asked me to help him try to get a better deal on a car. He asked me to call the seller, to go see it, and to offer a lower price on the car so he could then swoop in and get a better price than the seller originally listed.

"He's stuck on the price," Joe said, and he didn't want to fork over that much cash.

I remember I didn't feel good about the idea then—I knew it was deceptive. But I wanted to help a friend out, so I called the guy and went to see it, as Joe had asked. I pointed out a couple flaws on the car and made the seller a lower offer than what Joe wanted to buy the car for.

About a day or so later, Joe called the seller and made a deal with him. He ended up with a nice special-edition Ford Maverick Grabber.

I didn't feel good about the manipulation, but it wasn't against the law.

Back then, I thought manipulating a guy who's selling a car was the worst thing he was up to.

But on January 18, 1977, police believe Joe raped a 25-year-old woman in Sacramento. The woman's husband was out of town for business.

Again, the attacker took the woman's car and dumped it off not far away from the house. Police found it in an apartment complex about 1.5 miles from the house. The doors were locked, and the keys were missing.[24]

On January 24, 1977, a 25-year-old woman was attacked in Citrus Heights. She had friends over that night, and they all left shortly after midnight, leaving her home alone. Later that night, a man broke in, tied her up, and raped her. She waited about 15 minutes after he left her house before she untied herself and called for help.

On February 7, 1977, a 30-year-old woman was attacked in Carmichael, California, around 6:50 a.m. after her husband had just left for work and she was home alone with her daughter. Her husband had spotted a suspicious van outside, according to the arrest warrant, and had asked her to make sure the door was locked as he left. She walked through the house checking the doors, but when she turned around, a man stood in her home, pointing a gun at her. The man—allegedly Joe—tied up the woman and raped her.

A neighbor had told police that he saw a man climb over a fence along the cement drainage ditch that night. At the time, the neighbor didn't think much of it. After all, it was close to Del Camp High School, and kids were always up to something. But then the woman came out of her house, yelling, prompting neighbors to help.

Police learned the woman's family had been burglarized twice before. They'd also received two phone calls where the mystery person on the other line hung up.[25]

On February 16, 1977, the attacker shot an 18-year-old man in the abdomen near his home in Sacramento. The man's father was in the house when he heard a loud noise in the backyard. He went to check it out when he saw his son and the shadow of a man. The unknown man took off running toward the street. A neighbor heard the gunshots and tried to follow the attacker, according to the arrest warrant, but he got away.

On March 7, 1977, a 38-year-old woman fell asleep in her Sacramento home after spending the evening at a friend's house. Before she went to sleep, she told police, she had checked all the doors and windows to make sure they were locked. An assailant broke into her home and raped her. He got in by prying open a rear window, breaking the bottom piece of it in the process.

On March 18, 1977, police believe Joe attacked a 16-year-old girl in Rancho Cordova after she came home from work. Before she left for work, according to police, she had asked her sister to leave the kitchen and porch light on. When she got home, she noticed that only the kitchen and living room lights shone through the darkness. A white male with an estimated age of 25 to 35 was waiting inside, and he attacked her.

Her father and another person came to check on her when she didn't answer the phone. They found the girl inside the house, bound. They quickly untied her. According to the arrest warrant, investigators found pry marks on the back sliding-glass door. The door latch was broken in half. All three bedrooms in the house had been ransacked.[26]

On April 2, 1977, a 29-year-old woman was attacked in her Orangevale home after everyone had gone to sleep. According to the arrest warrant, there had been prowler activity and recent reports of burglary in the area. One homeowner reported chasing a man who fit the description of the East Area Rapist.[27]

On April 15, 1977, a 19-year-old woman who lived with her fiancé in Carmichael was raped. She woke up to a man shining a flashlight in her face, according to the warrant.

The man bound the woman and her fiancé, raped her, and took about $100 in cash. She eventually grabbed a knife from the kitchen and cut her bindings off before she went to free her fiancé. She never saw the man's face, but she noted he wore military style boots.

Investigators later learned nearby neighbors had reported a prowler standing by the window.

On May 3, 1977, a 30-year-old woman was raped in Orangevale while her husband and her two children were asleep in the house with her. According to the arrest warrant, their house backed up against the levee for the American River.

On May 14, 1977, another woman was raped in Citrus Heights. She too lived with her husband. The attacker bound her and her husband, raped the woman, and left.

Investigators learned that as with many of the other reports, people spotted a man prowling around about a month before the attack. Neighborhood kids reported seeing a stocky man walking through people's backyards.[28]

On May 17, 1977, a 26-year-old woman was raped in Carmichael. She was asleep in bed with her husband when the attacker broke in and woke them up.

On September 4, 1977, the East Area Rapist attacked a girl at her parents' house in Carmichael. She had gone over around 4 p.m. to do laundry there, according to the arrest warrant. Around 11:15 p.m., she was putting her laundry in her car, which was parked in front of the house. When she turned around, a man stood in front of her. He then raped her and took her car.[29]

Much of what happened in between was redacted in the arrest warrant, but the woman got free and contacted police. Bob Miller, sheriff's department spokesman in 1977, told the *Sacramento Bee*, "He was either waiting for the girl, or was there to burglarize the house."[30]

The house was a dark street with no overhead streetlights. A drainage ditch ran north of it and a nature area ran south of it. The house was also about 2.5 miles away from American River College, where I had once gone to school. It would have been less than 30 miles away from Auburn.

On September 6, 1977, the East Area Rapist made his way to Stockton, California, venturing out from the Sacramento area for one of the first known times.

Stockton is just under 85 miles away from Auburn.

CHAPTER 8

EAST AREA RAPIST CHECKS MY HOME SECURITY

According to *Napa Valley Register* archives, on September 6, 1977, a man in a ski mask attacked a 28-year-old woman in her home, binding the woman's husband then raping her twice. He lingered in the house for about 90 minutes, stealing jewelry and money.[31]

As the attacks continued, media coverage intensified.

At this point, the Sacramento County Sheriff's Department realized they were dealing with a serial burglar and rapist case. They noticed the suspect was targeting women in the California communities of Rancho Cordova, Arden/ Fair Oaks, Orangevale, and Citrus Heights.[32]

Joe, of course, was familiar with most, if not all, of these places. They're all within five to 20 miles east of Sacramento. His sister lived in Rancho Cordova. My mom and dad lived in Citrus Heights. Cindy and I lived in Orangevale.

By staying out of Auburn for the most part, he didn't risk people recognizing him going about his daily business.

He didn't risk local police getting too close for comfort. For a serial rapist, it was the perfect setup.

Two women were raped in Orangevale, near where Cindy and I lived with our little girl. We were scared and worried by the news.

One weekend in the spring of 1977, Joe rode up to my house on his motorcycle. When he pulled up, I was in the garage with the door open, a gas can in my hand, getting ready to mow the lawn. Joe popped off his helmet with his gloved hands and came in to catch up.

We talked about motorcycles, family, and the model boat I was working on. Then we started talking about the news— the East Area Rapist hadn't been caught, and people were scared. Some neighbors had put in custom floodlights, built fences, and installed wrought-iron bars on their windows. Others around the city bought revolvers and pistols to keep themselves and their families safe. Men patrolled their neighborhoods on foot and in cars to watch for nefarious behavior. Hardware stores ran out of door and window locks. People even got dogs to help guard their houses.

Cindy and I were scared, too. I bought a pistol after hearing about the crimes and kept it under my pillow at night, hoping I'd be able to protect my family if the East Area Rapist paid my house a visit. I'd heard about how the rapist would tie the men up and stack dishes on them, so he'd know if they tried to wriggle free to fight back.

I told Joe about the pistol and that the East Area Rapist would get a hell of a fight out of me. If I didn't kill him, I said, I'd hurt him so he'd get captured. I went on about how I thought the police response had been disappointing, how horrible it made women feel, and how wrong it seemed that one man could terrorize an entire city.

Joe played his role perfectly. He told me my home security was in good shape. I took him around the house to show him the window locks and sticks I put in the windows. With brotherly concern, he checked all the security adjustments I'd made. He told me what kind of strange sights and sounds I should pay attention to at night. He checked all the door locks to make sure they worked properly. He was a police officer and he was like my brother, so I trusted he knew what he was talking about.

"You have nothing to worry about," Joe said.

I felt relieved when he told me that. I felt a renewed sense of control and safety in my own home.

But now when I think back to that moment, my stomach drops. I showed Joe all the security measures I had taken to protect my family from *him*. He easily could have come for us. He's suspected of having committing at least 20 rapes by the time we had that conversation, some only blocks from my home. He was so careful not to show his dark side to me.

Now I can't help but wonder if my life or my kids' lives were in danger at some point. Are we only alive because he didn't want to be questioned about it? He could have killed me many times. Maybe he was capable of caring for people to some degree, like his kids, Sharon, and me.

I'll probably never know for sure.

I didn't see much of Joe or Sharon in 1978. The company I worked for, Terra Nova Produce, went bankrupt by November of 1977. In January I got hired on to inspect vegetables crossing the border. I followed the fruits and vegetables from Nogales, Arizona, to the Coachella Valley and all over the Southern California growing areas until I ended up in Stockton. I stayed in many motels during those days. It was a grind, but by summer I was a permanent part of the Stockton Snoboy produce team. We sold the house in Orangevale in September of 1978 and bought a house in Lodi, California, which is some 75 miles south of Auburn.

Sharon was busy studying for her law degree then. When we did see Sharon and Joe, it was at Mom and Dad's house when we all gathered to celebrate birthdays and holidays. My mom was that party person who loved to celebrate with everyone; it kept us connected even when life got busy.

Amid our family's celebrations, the attacks and killings continued, including 14 rapes in 1978, at least three of them involving teens. That was the same year that Brian and Katie Maggiore were killed as they walked their dog near Sacramento.

In January 1978, the East Area Rapist attacked two teenagers in their home just south of American River Community

College, where Sharon had attended school. When the girls' parents came home, they found their children tied up. The attacker was gone. The girls told police he wore a ski mask, carried a handgun, and had what looked like a knife.[33]

On February 2, 1978, a young husband and wife, Brian and Katie Maggiore, walked through Cordova Meadows, a quiet middle-class subdivision within Rancho Cordova, with their dog.

The East Area Rapist still frequented the area.

A neighbor told police he saw the attacker and the Maggiores run from his backyard into an adjacent yard through a section of the fence that had been blown down. He saw the attacker raise his arm and shoot at the two as they ran. They were taken to hospitals nearby but died from the gunshot wounds.

In the days and weeks leading up to the murders, 12 nearby homes experienced hang-ups or silent phone calls, burglaries, and prowling incidents.[34]

All the crimes had happened within a one-third mile radius of each other, according to law enforcement. Police went back through about 30,000 crime reports to narrow down the murderer's potential prior activity in the area.

A week before the murder, one woman told police she got a hang-up call every night around 8:00 p.m. The calls stopped the night the Maggiores died. Two other women in a separate household told police the same thing—the caller always called around 8:00 p.m.

A young couple who'd recently moved to the neighborhood had reported a prowler creeping around and a burglary in the winter of 1977 around Christmastime, according to police. The couple had come home to find the gates and doors open, but nothing had been taken.

A 25-year-old woman reported a prowler a little more than a month before the murders, according to police. She found shoeprints outside her bedroom window and noticed her gate was constantly being left open. When she tried to secure the gate, the prowler simply forced his way in, damaging the gate. She found drawings on the window, too, made from what appeared to be the prowler's bodily fluids, according to police.[35]

On March 14, 1978, police believe the East Area Rapist returned to Stockton to rape another woman. He woke up a 24-year-old woman and her husband, according to the *Los Angeles Times* archives. He tied up the man and took the woman to another room where he raped her twice.

He got in through a door with a broken lock.[36]

On April 14, 1978, another rape was reported in Sacramento. This time a 15-year-old babysitter was raped twice on a Friday night. She was watching an eight-year-old girl at the time. The girl was awake during the attack but didn't come out of her room. According to the *Times-Advocate* archives, a masked man kicked in the back door of the house while the girl watched television around 10 p.m. He wore gloves and possibly had a gun.[37]

According to the *San Francisco Examiner* archives, the younger girl's parents had telephoned the house, but no one answered. Concerned, they called the babysitter's parents, who lived nearby.

They called, and the girl answered with a "hello" and the phone hung up, according to the *Examiner*. So the babysitter's parents drove to the house. As they pulled into the driveway, the attacker escaped into the backyard and darkness.[38]

Police released a composite sketch of the killer in April of 1978.

The sketch depicts a young man with short, swooping hair, strong eyebrows, a square face, and a small smirk. The man in the drawing hardly looked threatening—he could have been any nice guy next door.

CHAPTER 9

"I'M GOING TO KILL THEM THIS TIME"

After the Maggiore murders, the East Area Rapist seemed to leave the Sacramento area. I was relieved for my family's sake. Life carried on for us.

According to police, the East Area Rapist moved on to the California cities of Modesto and Davis between June and July of 1978.

- On June 5, 1978, the East Area Rapist sexually assaulted a woman in Modesto.
- On June 7, 1978, a rape was reported in Davis.
- On June 23, 1978, there was another rape in Modesto.
- On June 24, 1978, there was a rape in Davis.
- On July 6, 1978, there was another rape in Davis.[39]

Joe was still working as an officer for the Auburn Police Department at the time. If he carried out the attacks in Modesto and Davis—and authorities allege he did—it's hard to imagine how he got any sleep. Modesto and Davis are located about 90 miles apart, and Auburn is located 115 miles from Modesto and 50 miles from Davis.

But his wife was buried in her studies. And I was struggling to provide for my family. I don't think he had anyone to keep track of what he was up to. I think Joe worked the swing shift back then as an officer anyway. I know he preferred working nights. He could be out all night, come home, and sleep until noon.

There was a three-month gap in East Area Rapist crimes after July 1978, according to police. The activity picked up again in October 1978. The East Area Rapist attacked two couples within two days of each other in Concord, California—located about 100 miles away from Auburn—in October 1978.

On October 28, 1978, he attacked again in San Ramon, California, about 115 miles from Auburn. According to the arrest warrant, the phone cord in the bedroom had been cut.

On November 4, 1978, he attacked a woman in San Jose, California. Joe would have traveled about 150 miles for this attack. It would have taken about 2.5 hours each way, depending on traffic conditions.

On December 2, 1978, he attacked another woman in San Jose.

On December 9, 1978, he attacked a woman in Danville, California. Police obtained a DNA sample after this attack.[40] Joe would have traveled another 120-some miles for this attack.

If I had to guess, I think he started wandering out further because the heat was on back home. Police were looking for him. People were afraid. Everyone seemed to be taking extra precautions.

In 1978, 15 victims got together for a luncheon to talk about their experiences after the attacks. Many of the women looked alike and came from similar backgrounds, according to the *San Francisco Examiner* archives. They were generally upper-middle class and had dark hair.[41]

I wasn't paying much attention to what Joe and Sharon were up to then. I was getting ready to sell my house in Orangevale. Cindy and I finally moved in September 1978. After I passed the trial period at my job in Stockton with Pacific Gamble Robins, Co., and became a permanent employee, we moved to Lodi. Lodi was much closer to my new job—about 20 miles. It didn't make sense to stay in Orangevale with such a big commute.

In 1979, Cindy decided she wanted to work and got a job at a dental office. We worked it out so I would drop Deanna off at daycare in the mornings, and either Cindy or I would pick her up.

In August that year, Joe got fired from the Auburn Police Department after he was charged with shoplifting.[42]

That October, a trial began to determine Joe's fate.

He apparently had tried to steal a hammer and dog re-pellant from a Pay 'n Save in Citrus Heights, just a few blocks from where my mom and dad lived. He got caught in the store with his pockets full. According to *Auburn Journal* archives, the dog repellant and the hammer were worth less than $20.

A store clerk testified he pulled the hammer from Joe's slacks after a struggle in the back room of the Pay 'n Save. The clerk told the court Joe was trying to escape during the struggle. When the Sacramento County Sheriff's deputies came to the store, Joe was tied to a chair, according to the *Journal*.[43]

Joe was suspended from duty with pay as city officials investigated the situation.

A jury found him guilty in October after a three-day trial. Joe came out of the incident with a misdemeanor, a $100 fine, and six months of probation, according to the *Journal*.[44]

He filed an appeal but dropped it in November 1979.

At the time, he told me he had put the items in his waistband, not to steal them, but to see if they'd fit. I didn't question it much. I thought maybe he planned to climb on the roof to do some repairs. I thought he was a good guy, so I believed him.

He also told me he wanted to kill his boss for payback after the police department let him go. People say things like that every day and I knew he was really upset—but I remember feeling a bit uneasy. It seemed like he meant it. I told him he was talking crazy.

All these decades later, I can't help but wonder if he had planned to carry those things in his waistband while he attacked people.

Joe said that he had gotten money in a settlement with the Auburn Police Department, and planned to use it to go to diesel truck repair school.

Before he got fired, he told me that he had gotten into deep shit with the department. He told me he was on his way to work one day; I don't remember what shift he was working, but it was dark outside. On his way to Auburn from his house, he saw a car in a ditch. He was in his private vehicle, he said, and had no cell phone or radio. He decided to head into work so he could tell dispatch about it. He said he didn't stop to check it out.

He said that he told dispatch about it, and when they sent someone over, it turned out to be a serious, major-injury accident. One of the victims was a councilmember's daughter.

He said he got hell for not stopping immediately. If it had been someone just needing a tow, he didn't think he would have gotten in trouble.

Now I don't know if that story is true. I don't know what to believe anymore.

Amid the workplace drama, authorities believe Joe still managed to rape at least six women, including two teenagers, murder a couple, and attempt to attack another couple.

On April 4, 1979, the East Area Rapist attacked a 27-year-old woman in Fremont, California. According to the *Los Angeles Times* archives, the woman's boyfriend was tied up and forced to lie face down on the floor as the attacker stacked dishes on his back.[45]

On June 2, 1979, he attacked a 17-year-old babysitter in Walnut Creek, California. The man was armed with a two-foot machete, according to *San Francisco Examiner* archives. The man came into the house through a rear sliding glass door and raped the girl while the two young children she babysat slept in another room.

On June 11, 1979, he attacked a 35-year-old woman in Danville. The East Area Rapist crawled through a window of a home near John Baldwin School, according to the article, tied up the woman's husband, and raped her. He wore a mask and flashed a pistol around. The couple's two daughters slept through the attack. That assault took place just blocks away from the December 9, 1978, attack in Danville. After the attack, Danville neighborhood residents began arming themselves and barring their doors.

Local locksmith Rich Carneolla told the *San Francisco Examiner* that his business tripled after the attack. "We've been installing 15 to 20 deadbolts a day," he said.[46]

But the deadbolt installations weren't enough. On June 25, 1979, he attacked another woman in Walnut Creek.

At the time, victims told police the worst part of the attacks wasn't the sexual act itself.

The rape "…lasted less than one minute and hardly ever resulted in serious physical injury," the *San Francisco Examiner* reported.

But he'd drag out the attack. He'd force his female victims to tie up their husbands with shoestrings or torn sheets. Then he'd stack dishes on top of the husband's bound body. If the man struggled or tried to escape while his wife was being raped, the attacker would know.

"I'll cut your toes off if you move," he told one victim, according to the *Examiner*. Victims described him as having a whispering voice. I don't remember Joe speaking in a whisper, but I have a feeling he wanted to mask the true sound.

The attacker was known for roaming around the house for up to two hours. He was known for going into the kitchen, taking a beer out of the fridge, and making himself at home.

A psychological profile commissioned during the 1970s suggested that the East Area Rapist "had a domineering mother and a weak or absent father, was an only child or maybe had a younger sister, and might be a paranoid schizophrenic. They also believed he went to college and [had] above-average intelligence."[47]

On July 6, 1979, the East Area Rapist tried to attack another woman in Danville. A woman woke up around 4 a.m. as a man wearing a ski mask tried to get through her window. She screamed and scared him off.

The July 6 attempt in Danville brought about the end of the known cases in Northern California. The attacker moved his target area to Southern California, which law enforcement now refers to as phase four of the attacks.

On October 1, 1979, weeks before the start of Joe's trial for the Pay 'n Save incident, a couple was attacked while they slept at their home in Goleta, California, which is in the Santa Barbara area. The woman told police she heard the intruder pacing back and forth repeatedly.

"I'm going to kill them," he said. "I'm going to kill them this time."

Frightened, she tried to run for the front door, but the attacker caught her. When the male victim heard her scream, he jumped out of bed. The attacker took off, leaving the scene on a stolen bike.

An off-duty FBI agent who was the couple's neighbor heard the commotion and got into his car to follow the attacker. The rapist got away, however, dropping the bike and hopping fences to escape.

On December 30, 1979, police believe Joe murdered Robert Offerman, an orthopedic surgeon and successful businessman, and Debra Manning, a successful psychologist. The two were found dead in Offerman's condo in Goleta, just north of Santa Barbara.[48] They were found by a friend of Offerman's who was supposed to meet him to play tennis around 11 a.m. that Sunday.

Manning was found naked, face down, with her hands tied behind her back. She died of a single gunshot wound to the back of her head, according to police. Offerman was found, also naked and bound, with three gunshot wounds—one to the top of the left buttock, one to the right side of his neck, and one to the front base of his neck.

Police determined he'd been shot with .38-caliber bullets, all fired from the same gun. Neighbors later told police that they may have heard gunfire around 3 a.m.

Capt. James Vizzolini, a detective on the case, told the *Santa Maria Times* that there had been reports of burglaries in the generally upper-middle-class complex. "We are making contact with everyone in the neighborhood and profiling all the other crime activities, collecting all kinds of physical evidence," Vizzolini told the *Times*.

In 1979, at least 27 people were killed in Santa Barbara County, an increase reflected in national trends, according to the *Times* archives.

"There are numerous theories on why the homicide rate is increasing," said John Carpenter, the Santa Barbara County sheriff in an interview with the *Times*. "One that has considerable merit is that people today tend to blame others more frequently for their problems and failures than themselves."[49]

Looking back, I suppose that does sound a bit like Joe. He was always a bit angry thinking about people who had more than he did. I think back to when he told me he'd let the guy who was speeding in a crappy car off with a warning while he'd give a guy in a nice car a ticket for speeding.

In 1980, my family started to fall apart. I learned that

Cindy had been having an affair with a guy from the Air Force base. We tried to work through it and work it out, but my dad told me things might never feel the same between us.

Joe and Sharon moved for work around 1979 or early 1980, at my best guess. I believe they had two residences in the early '80s, one near Los Angeles, where Sharon was working at the time, and one in Citrus Heights, where Joe lived. Joe easily could have made a pit stop in Ventura, about 70 miles north of the LA residence, on his way home from visiting Sharon. Investigators say he broke into Lyman and Charlene Smith's home in Ventura.

On March 16, 1980, Lyman Smith and his wife, Charlene Smith, were found dead in their home. Lyman was a former deputy district attorney who was expecting to be appointed as a judge by then-Governor Jerry Brown.

Lyman was found naked, face down on the right side of the bed, according to police. Both his hands and feet had been bound. Charlene was naked from the waist down, lying face up. Her hands were bound behind her back. Her ankles were also bound.

According to the *San Bernardino County Sun* archives, their bodies were found by Lyman's 12-year-old son, Gary, who came by to mow the lawn. At the time, he lived with his mom.[50]

The attacker had used a log from their firewood pile outside the house to beat them to death.

The house didn't appear to be ransacked, and nothing appeared to be stolen. Police were able to collect a semen sample. Years later, investigators found that it matched the East Area Rapist's DNA profile.[51]

It may have seemed strange to law enforcement then that the DNA was linked. After all, the East Area Rapist previously targeted folks mostly in the Sacramento area. For context, Sacramento is nearly 400 miles away from Ventura. But with the move to the Greater Los Angeles area, Joe was much closer.

On August 21, 1980, Keith and Patrice Harrington were found dead in their Laguna Niguel, California, home. Like many of the others before them, they were found in their bed. The two shared a house with Keith's father, Robert. Police noted the house was in a gated neighborhood, but anyone on foot could easily gain access to it.

Keith was a medical student at UC Irvine and Patrice was a nurse. According to the arrest warrant, they'd both been bludgeoned with a blunt object. Keith was found naked, while Patrice was found wearing a short, white terry cloth robe. Both had binding marks on their wrists.

Nothing seemed to be taken from the house.

"That there's no apparent motive is the saddest and most frustrating factor in their deaths," said Bruce Harrington, one of Keith's brothers, in an interview with the *Los Angeles Times*. "This was a senseless and apparently non-motivated crime."

"There would have been a degree of comfort if we could

say this was a robbery or that they had enemies. But they were warm and compassionate people; there is nothing in their background that can help us."[52]

Police were able to collect semen from that crime scene, too, and link it back to the East Area Rapist cases.

Laguna Niguel is about 40 miles or so from Long Beach. Under the right circumstances, Joe could have made it to the Harringtons' house from his in less than an hour.

CHAPTER 10

JOE HAS KIDS AND THE KILLER STOPS

In 1981, I learned that Cindy was pregnant with our second daughter, Nicole. It was around then that I started thinking back to what my dad had told me. Things between Cindy and me didn't feel the same. I couldn't shake the lingering betrayal I felt after her infidelity. I always had it in my mind that I'd rather be alone than be with the wrong person.

Also, the company I worked for decided to close all its buying operations in California. I had to figure out what to do when my company car and decent pay went away. I took on a job in Lodi with a local shipper that needed help for the summer to do what I could to provide for my family.

Life was a bit chaotic, and I didn't see much of Joe over the summer. A woman in Irvine, California, and a couple in Goleta were murdered in the months before the birth of Joe and Sharon's first baby girl.

On February 6, 1981, Manuela Whittuhn, 28, was found dead in her Irvine home. Manuela worked as a teller handling auto loans for the Airport Branch of the California First National Bank. Her husband, David, was in the hospital at the time of the attack.

Manuela was found dressed in a bathrobe, partially wrapped in a sleeping bag, according to the arrest warrant. She received multiple blows to the back of her head. As with the other victims, police found binding marks around her wrists and ankles.[53]

Police recovered semen from the scene. The DNA profile from that sample also matched up with the East Area Rapist.

David continued to get creepy phone calls for 30 years after his wife's death.

"We would get calls, creepy breathing calls," Rhonda, David's second wife, said in an interview. "One time we had a call where he said, 'I'll kill you,' or 'I'm going to kill you!'"

David and Rhonda moved to escape the horrifying taunts. David died in 2008 of natural causes.

When Rhonda heard Joe's voice after his 2018 arrest, she believed it was the very same one that haunted her and David for years, she told the *Toronto Sun*.[54]

On July 27, 1981, Greg Sanchez and Cheri Domingo were found dead in a Goleta home.

Cheri was house-sitting that night. Her teenage daughter had been house-sitting with her, but she happened to be at a friend's house that night, according to the *Santa Maria Times* archives.[55] The owner of the house had died earlier that year, and his heirs had put the house up for sale.

Police described Greg as Cheri's boyfriend, though according to the *Times*, they'd recently broken up and were good friends. He was an engineering technician. Greg had come over to visit Cheri that night. Both were bludgeoned to death. Detectives described the murders as "brutal."

According to the *Los Angeles Times* archives, neighbors told police they had heard loud bangs and a scream around 3 a.m., but they ignored it, thinking someone had set off fireworks.

When real estate agents arrived to inspect the property, they found the victims' bodies.

Greg was found naked, face down on the floor. He was partly inside the bedroom closet. Police discovered he had one non-fatal gunshot wound that came in through his left cheek. However, the 24 blows to his head were fatal. Police didn't find any binding marks.

Cheri was found naked, lying face down in the bed, her body completely covered. Both of her arms were behind her back; police found binding marks on her wrists. Cheri died from multiple blunt force injuries to her head.

Detectives were convinced the murders were related to the homicide involving Robert Offerman and Debra Manning. After all, these more recent murders had taken place about three blocks away from the others.[56]

According to the *Lompoc Record* archives, two Neighborhood

Watch meetings were held in Goleta in the weeks after the murders. More than 100 people showed up.

Police got more than 80 requests to inspect homes and give advice on security, something that normally happened five to 10 times per week.

Santa Barbara County saw at least 23 homicides in 1981.

A couple of other homicides grabbed headlines that year. Santa Barbara sculptor Giovanni Schoeman, his business partner Cornelis Moll, and Schoeman's friend, Kimberly Roberts, were killed "execution style," according to the *Record*. Apparently diamond smuggling was the motive.

Another murder centered around a deadly love affair at remote Ogilvy Ranch, where Lewis Price was charged with shooting James Howell and burning his body after he began intruding on Price's blossoming romance with a woman named Gina Savio.

Those murders were horrible in their own right—but at every turn there seemed to be a reason why they happened, however convoluted it was. The East Area Rapist attacked without any apparent rhyme or reason. He could have gone after anyone. I think that's what scared people the most.[57]

Disconnected from the horrific murders of Greg Sanchez and Cheri Domingo, I celebrated as Joe and Sharon's first daughter, Misha, was born in September. Sharon would bring Misha over to Mom's house, and Mom would invite us to come over. I'd stop by to see them.

I believe Sharon had a job with the National Labor Relations Board then. Joe didn't talk much about work. I can't recall what or if he did anything more than helping with Misha during the period when authorities believe he was committing a gruesome wave of violent acts.

We spent most holidays together at Mom and Dad's house. On Christmas, we all spoiled our kids. Mom and Dad always put up a fully decorated six- or seven-foot tree in the house where we grew up. Years earlier, Dad took one of the walls out completely, making for a giant room. He had a bookshelf built into the wall, and he turned it into a library.

Cindy and I were affectionate, especially in the early years of our marriage. I'd give her a kiss in the hallway or a pat on the butt. That seemed normal to me. But when I did anything like that, Joe would just go off on me.

"No PDA," he would say.

"What do you mean?" I asked.

"No public displays of affection."

I'd never heard the term until he used it, but I heard it from him a few times. I kind of stopped doing things like hugging my wife when he was around. I didn't want to deal with the fuss it would cause. I don't recall seeing him hug his children, though it was clear he loved them. He never really hugged my kids either. I never saw him and Sharon touch while they were together.

My kids got lots of hugs, and when Joe wasn't around,

I wasn't shy about showing Cindy affection. I thought Joe's desire for privacy was a little strange. People have different ways of interacting with each other.

Within months of Nicole being born, Cindy started talking about having a third child, but I wasn't feeling it. Everything had changed with the affair. Around March 1982, I moved into an apartment; soon after, Cindy filed for divorce. We worked it out so I could have my girls every other weekend, Friday evening to Sunday evening.

I got a job that year with General Produce. It was a good job and the pay was decent. I worked about 54 hours each week, commuting after the divorce until Mom and Dad helped me buy a house on Freeway Circle in Sacramento.

All the hard work paid off for Sharon. She was admitted to the State Bar of California in 1982.

I took Deanna to visit. We went to Disneyland, and later we took Misha and Deanna to Knott's Berry Farm. I think Misha was around two years old and Deanna was seven.

Sharon was busy working, and Joe wasn't around. I don't know what he was busy with at the time. Being a father of two little girls and settling into a new job took up most of my attention then, so looking back, my memory is a bit sketchy on what was happening with Joe and Sharon between 1981 and 1986.

Around 1986 or 1987, Joe and his family moved to their Canyon Oaks home in Citrus Heights. Sharon got a job working for the State of California. She wasn't there for long—she thought it was too political. Eventually she started up her own practice as a divorce attorney, work she was doing at the time of his arrest.

With them being so close in Citrus Heights, I'd visit them often, usually with my girls in tow. On weekends I worked until 11 a.m. on Saturdays, so they helped me out by watching the girls Friday night until about noon Saturday, keeping them entertained.

Joe and Sharon's second daughter, Sascha, had been born in November 1986 while they were in Southern California. Just months before Sascha arrived, the Golden State Killer committed his last known crime. It was tragic and horribly violent.

Janelle Cruz,18, worked as a cashier for a Bullwinkle's Pizza. She was home alone on May 4, 1986, when she encountered the notorious attacker in her home in Irvine. According to a report by *Oxygen*, her sister, Michelle Cruz, said, "he bound her, raped her, and bludgeoned her beyond recognition."

Her body was found by real estate agents. Janelle's mom was on vacation in Mexico at the time.

Despite the crime showing telltale signs of the East Area Rapist, police initially arrested the wrong man.

Gregory Gonzalez, who had met Janelle in a drug rehabilitation class, told someone he'd killed her. It wasn't until later that they discovered the DNA profile matched up with the East Area Rapist.

"I wasn't looking for another suspect because it appeared to me to be Greg Gonzalez," said Larry Montgomery, who worked on the case, to the *Los Angeles Times*.[58]

As far as authorities can tell, that was the Golden State Killer's last crime. Once again, authorities found that the DNA matched the East Area Rapist's profile—they just didn't yet know who he was.

CHAPTER 11

FAMILY LIFE AND GROWING RAGE

Deanna and Nicole enjoyed going over to see their cousins. We went over to see them just about every third or fourth weekend. Joe and Sharon had a Doughboy pool in their backyard set up for the kids. It rose out of the ground about three or four feet, surrounded by Joe's well-manicured green lawn. The kids spent hours splashing around while we'd barbecue. We'd cook up hot dogs for the kids and hamburgers for the grown-ups. The kids came out only when the food was ready, and their fingers looked like prunes.

Every now and then, Joe would hop in and play Marco Polo in the pool with the kids. They'd take turns closing their eyes and shouting out to each other, giggling and splashing around under the hot California sun. I got in to play with them all a few times, too.

Sometimes Deanna and Nicole would join forces with their cousins to have water balloon fights with the neighbor kids in the summer. They'd carefully fill up each balloon, neatly tying up the plastic tail just to lob it over at the other kids. They'd squeal and laugh as the other kids returned fire, balloons bursting on the hot concrete. Colorful, rubbery pieces left a telltale sign of the destruction up and down the driveway.

Every morning after the girls spent the night, Joe diced up potatoes to make his signature hash browns or breakfast fries. He chopped them up so quickly his hands were a blur. There were mere milliseconds between thwacks on the cutting board.

When Nicole was a youngster, she wondered if Joe lost the tip of his finger cutting potatoes so fast. When she asked, Joe and I would tell her he lost it in the war, but she was skeptical. For years, she thought it was a battle scar from breakfast.

Joe had an affinity for model boats, and we spent hours building them just for fun. We started with the slower boats, then Joe went on to build faster ones. Joe got into model airplanes soon after. He built the Shelley Foss Tug, a model kit about three feet long, then he built a destroyer-style boat on a smaller scale.

I remember he mentioned that he thought it would be cool to put an actual gun in the turret of his boat so he could fire it, but to my knowledge he never followed through with the idea. Joe liked guns and had many, and he was also into reloading back then. I know that over the years he must have bought and sold many guns.

I shot a .44 Magnum once, but it wasn't Joe's. I held it

with two hands, but the recoil still threw the gun-hammer so far back it nearly hit my forehead. In later years, Joe encouraged his youngest daughter to practice firing his .44. It was a bit too much for her to handle at the time. He knew this, so he packed the cartridges with half the amount of powder before he let her try.

Many hunters and gun enthusiasts make custom rounds. I know Joe liked to have control over the cartridges he created. The only reason he ever gave me for this was adjusting the recoil for his daughter to practice firing rounds. But I realize now that making custom bullets also made them less traceable.

Looking back, I also realize that he may have alluded to his crimes at least once. I wish I would have paid more attention then.

"I know how to get rid of someone," he told me. It wasn't a specific threat, but he insinuated he knew how to get away with murder.

I shrugged it off then. *Of course, he'd know something like that*, I thought. He'd spent years in the military and law enforcement. I thought he was just bragging, in his own strange way. Maybe, I thought, it made him feel more like a man. I also knew he was prone to exaggeration and enjoyed telling tall tales from time to time.

He'd tinker with cars in the garage, too. His pride and joy was the Bel Air, a Chevy wagon. It worked as a family wagon with tons of torque that hauled our kids around with ease. It was low and wide; its big bed was more than wide enough to accommodate his carefully made model boats and planes.

In 1980, he sold me his 1950 Chevy Deluxe sedan. He'd worked on it continually before he took to working on the Bel Air. I commuted with that big, bulbous car for more than a year! But I didn't have the enthusiasm Joe had for constantly working on cars, and the old ones required a lot of attention. I sold the Deluxe in 1983.

For all the fun we had with Joe, he had his bad moments. Every so often he'd start ranting and raving about the keys he had misplaced.

"Where are my fucking keys?" he'd yell until he found them.

He would just go nuts. Any time he started yelling, we knew what it was about, so we'd help him look for the damn keys. He'd find them eventually, or one of us would. Then he'd just set them on the washing machine or somewhere, but never in the same place where he might actually find them again. It didn't bother us too much. It was just one of those things Joe did, and we were used to it.

There were moments, too, when he lost his cool, shouting at the model airplanes he worked on in his garage. Sometimes he'd yell like hell at the girls for misbehaving, though it could be hard to judge what he'd deem to be punishment-worthy.

Once, Nicole and Misha were picking on Sascha, Joe's second born. They ran around poking fun at her weight. Joe went off on them both. He sat Nicole down in the living room next to the desk and told her not to go anywhere. Then he gave Misha a verbal licking.

Joe yelled a lot, so it seemed normal most of the time. But Nicole remembers being scared of him that day he yelled at her. Maybe normal people wouldn't have reacted with such venom and force, or maybe he was a protective father who had hit his limit.

Many neighbors later told media outlets they knew Joe as a little odd but generally friendly. Some had a different impression. Grant Gorman, who was a kid in the '90s, when he lived behind Joe, said Joe left an anonymous voicemail on his family's answering machine threatening to kill his dog. Gorman's dad recognized Joe's voice right away.

"[The message] said, 'If you don't shut that dog up, I'll deliver a load of death,'" Gorman told ABC News.

Gorman said Joe could be paranoid and sometimes accused the other kids of spying on him, throwing things at the house, or being on his property. He didn't hold back from yelling and cursing across the yard, giving the little boys on the other side of the fence a good scare.[59]

Sometimes he'd egg on Nicole to curse, too, even before her teenage years. Nicole went through a phase where she'd say, "Goddamn it," all the time, and it would crack Joe up.

"Say it again," he said, and she would. This occurred while I wasn't around, Nicole told me.

"Nicole, you're so funny," he would say, laughing along.

Joe often told stories as he took them out to get pizza. For example, he'd tell them a story about a boy who would pick his scabs and eat them. Nicole doesn't remember the name of the boy, but Joe was fond of that story. He told it many times. The girls laughed a bit, telling him he was gross. But he just laughed along.

Joe could be particular about how he did things. He typically wore a white T-shirt and shorts, for example. He rarely integrated color into his wardrobe. He liked that look, so he stuck with it.

He also had a certain way he wanted things done around the house. He insisted the doors always be shut and the dishes done, possible remnants from his days in the Navy. The girls knew they'd catch hell if they got too messy, but that didn't always stop them.

Joe wasn't big on holidays, but every year he set up Easter baskets for his kids. Every year it was the same thing. He'd reuse the same baskets, packing them full of chocolate bunnies and other Easter candies.

He put a lot of work into keeping up his yard. Joe preferred the girls play in the driveway, in the pool, or across the street in the neighbor's grass. Sometimes neighbors spotted him trimming the grass around the two huge boulders in his yard with scissors, ensuring the perfect cut.

When Nicole stayed the night, Joe insisted she sleep in a

room separate from Misha. However, sometimes he'd set up a tent in the living room they could share. He never told Nicole why this was his rule, and I didn't know about it until later. It's normal for girls to sleep in the same room or even the same bed during sleepovers. It's not something I ever thought twice about with my own kids when they had friends over. Nicole wonders if Joe wanted to keep an eye on them. His room was near the kids' rooms, and he could probably hear most of what went on.

When they were kids, Nicole remembers Joe would be upset if she or Misha would play around, jumping out of the bath naked. He'd yell at them to get their clothes on.

Unless Nicole had permission to use his shower, Joe's room was off-limits. None of the kids dared to break that rule. When Nicole did use the shower, Joe gave her specific instructions on cleaning up afterward. So far, the FBI has been mum on exactly what they confiscated from Joe's house. The inventory of what the FBI found in Joe's house is still under lock and key.

Weekends with Joe back then were filled with familiar patterns. We often went to get a pizza. There was one pizza parlor in particular we frequented. Joe liked to get extra sauce on his pizza, and this place did it just the way he liked. We'd bring the pizza with us and stop by Blockbuster to grab a movie to watch that night. It was the kids, Joe, and me. Sharon was typically locked away in her room, working on various cases and building up her law practice. She was around, but she didn't participate much.

We'd all gather to watch horror movies with characters like Pumpkinhead, Freddy Krueger, Jason, or Chucky. The kids liked getting scared. It was like a little party at Joe's house. He'd even make up stories about the boogeyman to give the girls a good scare.

Many of the horror movies we watched were fantasy. A killer doll was scary, sure, but it wasn't rooted in reality. One time we rented *The Texas Chainsaw Massacre*, an American slasher film that came out in 1974. It follows the story of a group of friends who encounter a hitchhiker with deadly intentions; gore and horror ensue.

The character Leatherface was loosely based on Ed Gein, a Wisconsin farmer who robbed graves, allegedly engaged in necrophilia and cannibalism, and murdered at least two women in the 1950s. One woman was found hanging naked, decapitated and disemboweled in Gein's home, according to a report by Snopes.

As we watched the movie, Joe's eyes opened wide and he seemed to disconnect from everyone else in the room. He clenched his teeth and talked through them. Later, I'd learn that's how the Golden State Killer talked to his victims.

The FBI released a recording of a 1977 phone call in which the Golden State Killer taunted a woman on the other line. The woman was one of the victims left alive. Authorities tapped her phone, knowing the Golden State Killer had a habit of calling before and after the attacks.

On the recording, you can hear unnerving heavy breathing. It seems to quicken in pace, becoming more aggressive.

"Gonna kill you... gonna kill you... gonna kill you," a man's voice says in a low, growling whisper. "Bitch. Bitch. Bitch. Bitch. Bitch. Fucking whore."[60]

When I listened to the recording years later, it made my skin crawl. It sounded a lot like Joe. As I heard the recording played on true crime shows after the arrest, I felt sure it could have been him.

I wonder now if Joe had been thinking of his crimes while we watched those slasher films together. Of course, normal people experience powerful emotions while they watch horror flicks—that's partly why we watch them. But usually we identify with the victim. We feel vulnerable and afraid. Looking back, I think Joe identified with the bad guys. I think he identified with feeling powerful.

When it was just the kids, Joe didn't stick around to watch the horror movies. Sometimes he'd look on for a moment while standing in the kitchen, but he'd head out to the garage after a while to do some work. He was always busy fiddling with things and fixing things, often working on his next model boat or plane.

Sometimes he'd give them a hard time for watching *Friday the 13th* so often.

"You guys are sick. You like that stuff?" he'd ask jokingly.

He'd often let the girls stay up as late as they wanted. Nicole and Misha stayed up all night watching movies and eating candy and popcorn, eventually falling asleep on the couch. Joe would cover the girls with blankets as he either got home from work late or left for work early.

Despite his affinity for horror films, he'd steer his daughters away from watching any true crime stories, especially on the news. If the girls landed on a true crime show while flipping through the channels, he'd comment on it.

"Why are you watching that crap?" he'd ask.

While the girls loved a good scare back then, Joe also acted as a protector if things got a little too real. Nicole once told him she was scared someone was going to break into the house while she was over there. She may have been freaked out because of all the scary movies, or maybe she was worried because we had our own break-in scare.

My house was burglarized in the mid-1980s. It happened on a Friday while I was picking up my daughters from their mom's house in Lodi. When we pulled up to our house, sheriff's deputies were there, already inside my home. Confused, I asked them what was going on. They told me a high school boy had seen some bad guys hauling stuff from my property and down the street. Either the boy or his parents called it in and reported the guys. Officers found the thieves in a motel near my house.

They asked me to take a look around and see what was missing. I don't remember everything they took, but for some reason I do remember they tried to run off with my TI business analyst calculator. They had it in the motel with them, and I got it back.

My fence backed up to a ditch and then a street running behind a commercial area on Madison Avenue. It made for a quick, though poorly executed, getaway. The method was eerily similar to the way the Golden State Killer used ditches to target his victims and escape from authorities.

But when Nicole was scared, Joe took her outside to show her how well protected the house was.

"There's nothing to be afraid of, I have it locked up real good," Joe said. The sliding glass door was double locked, and the other doors were barricaded. He took his own home security very seriously. It made Nicole feel better and safer then.

Joe could be a bit of a penny-pincher, too.

He wanted the air-conditioning unit to be militantly controlled, never running all day. He was strict about turning the lights off, too. He also tried to get the best deals on pizza when he could. And he always told the girls not to waste their food. I later learned he wouldn't make quite enough for them to be wasteful.

When Misha would ask for extra soda, Joe would get on her case for drinking too much in a day.

Sometimes he'd sneak the girls into drive-in movies, using

the expansive space of the Bel Air to go undetected. He'd tell them to get in the back and hide, throwing a blanket over them so he wouldn't have to pay for them to get in. They'd stop by the grocery store beforehand and load up on candy and snacks, so they could get the goods for cheaper than they would at the drive-in.

It was another one of Joe's shenanigans—he didn't pay attention to rules unless he had to. Most of the time it seemed innocent enough. But I did hear about a couple instances I didn't approve of years later.

Nicole later told me Joe would take them to a park near the house at night, even when it was closed. They would climb on the monkey bars and go down the slide, climbing all over the playground. The girls played together and had a blast as they giggled and squealed.

Nicole remembers feeling happy and free on those nights. She thought it was so cool. No one else was around, and only stars and streetlights cut through the darkness. It wasn't something I would have let them do had I been there. I know parks close at night, and I like to respect those rules.

Joe also let the kids run amok in the grocery store. He'd take them to pick up snacks and food for the morning. Sometimes he let them wander down the refrigerated section—all riled up as kids get when they're together—to pour milk out on the floor. One of the girls popped open a carton and dumped it out, the chilled white liquid cascading onto the floor with a *glug, glug, glug.*

He laughed when he caught them in the act before he said, "Let's get out of here." But he didn't punish them for it. Sometimes he'd even encourage misbehavior.

On the Fourth of July, Joe would go all out. He bought all kinds of fireworks, big and small. The girls lit sparklers in the driveway for some harmless fun. But Joe also encouraged them to put smoke bombs in the mailbox or put ground spinners under cars.

As far as I know, the neighbors never complained. It was just another example of Joe pushing the limits of appropriate behavior.

My girls knew they would have been in trouble if I'd known about the shenanigans, so they didn't tell me about it when they were kids. I learned about it all years later when we rehashed everything we knew about Joe in light of the DNA evidence pointing to him as the Golden State Killer.

It makes me wonder what else he could have done with my kids or to them without my knowing about it. Did anything happen that they don't remember so many years later? Did he touch my children? Both my daughters say he didn't. But I have to live with knowing I left them alone with someone now accused of raping and killing girls not much older than they were.

CHAPTER 12

THE HIDDEN BAR OF GOLD

In early 1988, I left my job at General Produce to work for competitor Lucky Fruit and Produce. It was basically the same job but with a different company. Soon, tensions erupted between the two companies. The owner of General Produce was pissed Lucky Fruit and Produce hired me away, so it hired away another employee as retaliation. Produce prices got lowered and started an all-out war. In the end, I got fired.

By then, I'd become a semi-regular at Peppermill, a restaurant in Sacramento, which was on my way home. I first started going there about the time I was newly divorced. It was a nice place to stop in and have a beer or two. One night, I met Steve there. He told me about his new job at Radio Shack. He asked me what I was doing for a living.

Once I told him I'd been fired, he told me I should apply for a job at Radio Shack. He went on about how he would be a store manager in a few months. Best of all, he said, retail was a lot of fun.

I decided some money was better than no money and gave it a try. It took me about a year or so to become a store manager, but Steve was right—it was fun. I managed for more than a decade after that. I did well, winning many manager-of-the-month and other awards.

I ended up leaving Radio Shack. It was a stressful job, I was losing interest, and the business underwent some serious changes. I switched to driving a truck to finish out my career. It suited me well. The difference in the stress levels was night and day. I had no employees to manage or sales numbers to beat. I could just do my job, do it well, and go home. I hopped jobs a lot, but to be honest, I never worked a job I was passionate about, so it didn't matter to me all that much.

I really loved flying, though. I loved the freedom that came with being up in the sky, flying around with the birds, flying near them but not chasing them. But flying just didn't happen for me career-wise. With the chaos of having young kids, the divorce, and finding a new job, I had taken a break from flying recreationally. I finally got back into it in June of 1987.

According to my flight logs, I took Joe up a couple times in 1987. In August, I took him up in a Cessna 172 for a night flight. It was a short night flight, mostly made up of the takeoff and landing. It was a fun way for him to experience a bigger plane. Plus, we got to fly up among the stars and take in the view of the city lights down below.

In October, I flew Joe and his brother, John, to Exeter in a Cessna 182. Joe had asked me what it would cost to make the trip. He wanted to drop his brother off so they wouldn't have to drive. Their sister still lived in Exeter, so I didn't think much of it. It was a nearly two-hour flight. We landed and then briefly went up again, touching back down to drop John off before heading home.

During the flight, I remember Joe seemed amazed at it all. It wasn't his first time in the air, but he was fairly quiet, taking it all in. It wasn't a big deal to me after the hundreds of hours I had spent flying, but at the time I was glad he seemed to enjoy it.

Joe had told me he wanted to give John a ride and avoid the long drive down to see his sister. But now I wonder if he was starting to get nervous about DNA evidence, which had just begun to be used in criminal cases. Maybe he was worried he might get pulled over by the same cop that he'd been accused of shooting at in Visalia.

According to the *Visalia Times Delta*, Joe had shot at Visalia officer Bill McGowen in December 1975, hitting his flashlight. McGowen, according to the report, "came inches away" from the shooter's face before he fired.

McGowen was staking out a home after a 19-year-old woman told police someone was peeping into her bedroom. McGowen, according to Joe's 2018 arrest warrant, spotted the prowler peeping through the window during his stakeout.

McGowen chased the guy, who'd removed his ski mask. It was sitting on top of his head but not covering his face.

The peeper looked at McGowen and begged him not to hurt him, according to the arrest warrant. He had one hand up over his head, the other in his jacket pocket. Joe quickly whipped out a handgun and fired at the officer. The bullet embedded in the flashlight's battery, and the force knocked McGowen backward. Joe made his escape hopping over a fence.[61]

McGowen may have recognized Joe if he saw him again.

When I look at the sketch based off McGowen's description, I think it looks a lot like Joe.

The sketch depicts a man with thin, swooping hair, almond-shaped eyes, and a wide, roundish face.

Joe might have just wanted to go up in the plane to give his brother a thrill. But I can't help but feel like he used me to get what he wanted and avoid trouble.

One day, maybe in 1988 or 1989, the kids were playing at Joe and Sharon's house and Joe called me into the garage.

"Let me show you something," he said.

He reached down underneath Sharon's antique white stove, which had been my grandma's until she died. He grabbed a towel and pulled it out from under the stove. He started unrolling and unraveling it with his back toward me.

He swung around and held out a gold-colored bar. I reached my hand out, and he just let it go. I caught it, but my hand dropped—I was surprised by the weight of it. That's when I realized he'd just dropped real gold into my hands. He looked at me mischievously.

It was about the size of a small TV remote. It looked like it had been cast in a teeny bread pan. I'd worked in metal fabrication at one point, so I knew about how much copper, aluminum, and steel weighed. Joe knew this. Gold's weight is twice what steel's is. This was another one of his shenanigans; I think he enjoyed the look of surprise that must have come over my face.

"It's pure 24 karat," he said.

If memory serves, he showed me a bar of the precious metal and several small puddles of gold possibly weighing five pounds or so. According to USAGOLD, an organization that tracks the price of gold, one ounce of the stuff went for around $483 at its peak in 1988.

"Where'd you get it?" I asked.

Joe told me he had gathered it while he served in Vietnam. Other sailors were always short on money when they'd go to shore, he told me, so he'd lend them five dollars or 10 dollars and then collect seven dollars or 14 dollars to make a profit for this short-term loan. He said he used the extra cash to buy single-ounce gold Krugerrands, which is a popular gold coin from South Africa. Joe told me he melted down the coins and recast them.

I asked him why he kept something that valuable under

the stove instead of in a safe. He told me he didn't want to keep his valuables in a place a burglar would be looking.

Back then, I was enamored with the gold. You could buy a house with what he kept wrapped up under the stove.

California District Attorney investigator Erika Hutchcraft said the killer usually took some kind of memento from the houses he terrorized.

"Something that would be significant to the victim, maybe a class ring or maybe a ring that a wife had given a husband that had his initials on it," Hutchcraft said. "Sometimes photos would be torn in half and he would take half the photo. He's able to prolong that crime by messing with the victim."

Now I think that what Joe said about the slush fund and the sailors needing cash was only half the story. I think his stash of gold was made partly from the jewelry he stole from his victims.

According to the search warrant issued by the Sacramento District Attorney's Office before the arrest, the Golden State Killer is accused of stealing many valuables and oddities.

For example, he stole:

- One size-6.5 orange blossom 14-karat gold woman's wide-band ring, inscribed with a name and the date "2/11/71"
- One size-9.5 orange blossom 14-karat gold man's regular band ring, inscribed with a name and the date: "2/11/71"

- One class ring, 14-karate white gold with white stone, inscribed with "Modesto Junior College 1970"
- One man's gold wedding band, inscribed with "For My Angel" along with the date "1/11/70"
- A .357 Magnum revolver
- A high school photograph of one of the victims
- One ladies' bathrobe
- One ring with two pearls, 10-karat gold
- Drivers' licenses
- Bus pass IDs
- Social Security cards[62]

Authorities wondered for years what the Visalia Ransacker and the Golden State Killer did with all the trinkets he stole. I think Joe melted down what he could and hid it in plain sight, much like he did himself. I don't know what he did with the rest. I don't remember seeing IDs that didn't belong to him laying around the house. Following Joe's arrest, I told the District Attorney's office about that day in the garage.

I wonder if Joe ever stole from me. I had a ring that went missing around 2000. It had a diamond and a bloodstone. I had it before I even met Cindy, but I didn't wear it often. I kept it in a little jewelry box. When I noticed it was missing, I thought Deanna's boyfriend at the time might have swiped it. Now I wonder if Joe stole that, too.

I wonder about a lot of things now. I can't help but turn scenarios like that over and over in my head. What other things did he steal? Did he hurt anyone close to me, and I just don't know it? Was my life in danger at any point? He could have killed me many times. He could have made it look like a hunting accident. It makes me wonder if he chose not to attack me or my family simply because it would have been easier for police to track him down. Were we nothing but a cover story to him?

I ignored some of the things about Joe that bothered me, because for a long time, I thought Sharon was happy. I didn't want to think about Joe in any kind of negative way, because we were family. I didn't want to upset my sister or my parents by bringing up little things I thought didn't matter then.

I think Joe knew that. I think he counted on Sharon and me to trust each other's judgment.

He made me doubt everything.

CHAPTER 13

THE BREAKUP

Joe and Sharon gradually drifted apart after they had children, separating in 1991.

They evidently slept in separate beds, I learned from media reports following his arrest. If this is true, I would guess it probably started so she could study half the night for law school and the bar exam without being disturbed by Joe. She didn't want to be distracted, and she was sensitive to noise.

In the late 1980s and early 90s, as their marriage fell apart, Sharon made national headlines for her work with the National Coalition Against Surrogacy, which worked to outlaw the practice of married couples paying other women to have their babies.

The organization sprang into action following the infamous "Baby M" case in which a New Jersey woman, Mary Beth Whitehead, was forced to give up her baby after giving birth. Sharon's efforts contributed to the enactment of laws banning paid surrogacy in Oregon, Washington, and maybe a dozen other states.

She'd worked with the coalition since before she and Joe split up. She worked fiercely to advocate for and protect her clients.

Despite the split, Sharon and Joe didn't file divorce paperwork.

Joe seemed to like their arrangement. He continued to tell people he was married to a lawyer. I think he liked the status that came with being associated with someone in a field like that. It was a big deal back then for a woman to break into the legal profession. In the 1970s, when Sharon began to pursue her dream career, women were still largely unwelcome in courtrooms. By the 1990s, the bias had started to lessen, but it was still a prestigious, unusual thing for women to have their own practices. I know my whole family was proud of Sharon and her work and achievements.

Sharon went with it. She wanted to do everything she could for the benefit of her children, including maintaining a relationship with their father. But she suspected he intentionally did things to annoy her. She suspected he used the children as pawns to keep an eye on her.

As their relationship deteriorated, I asked her what had happened between them. She didn't give me any specifics, but I recall that she said he was manipulative.

Sharon finally filed for divorce in 2018. Many media outlets and internet sleuths have speculated it's because Sharon knew something about Joe's crimes, but it's a lot simpler than that. Joe had very good health insurance and Sharon needed to keep her insurance. By not filing the paperwork, Sharon got to keep her health insurance for free, and Joe still got to say he was married to a lawyer.

The pending divorce could have significant ramifications in Joe's upcoming trial. With the divorce filing, the DA's office can subpoena her and compel her to testify, attorney Mark Reichel told KTXL. She won't be able to talk about specific conversations or communication she had with Joe, but she'll be able to testify on her observations, such as what clothes he was wearing or if she noticed anything suspicious.

Joe and Sharon never seemed to fight when I was around, but neighbors told a different story once Joe was arrested. According to a report by the *Mercury News*, neighbors witnessed Joe and Sharon getting into "epic shouting battles." One neighbor described Joe as "unstable" with a "really bad temper." According to the report, the neighbor forbade his kids from playing with Joe's children.[63]

In Misha's teenage years, Joe and Misha would get into big fights. Nicole could hear him yelling at her over the phone. Misha would tell her Joe was a madman, that she was afraid of him.

Nicole wasn't sure what to think of it all. She had a feeling something wasn't right with how they interacted, but some of it seemed like teenage rebellion, too. Misha wasn't always nice to Joe either. She dated people Joe didn't want her to date and did things he didn't want her to do. Nicole figured he was just trying to be a good dad, even if he went overboard at times.

I didn't see that part of it. They kept it together pretty well when dealing with the family. When they first split, I asked Sharon if I should cut ties with Joe. He'd become such an integral part of my kids' lives and mine, it felt wrong to simply pick sides. Sharon said she didn't mind if we remained friends, so we did.

We went shooting a handful of times. On our last trip, we took shotguns out to shoot clay. I told Joe about a place at the Bear River I'd tried before. It also came recommended by a friend who knew a thing or two about good places to shoot. I think this was around 2008.

The Bear River runs some 73 miles through California. The water touches rocky crags that jut out toward the sky. It's a beautiful area teeming with life.

Joe drove us out there. I remember his being apprehensive about the place. He wasn't familiar with it. It was out of his routine.

On the way, we stopped in town to get a couple sodas. Joe spotted a local police officer and began chatting with her. Being a bit unfamiliar with the location, Joe wanted to make sure we were shooting in an area where it was legal, which was a noticeable shift from his days hunting illegally with his ex-fiancé, Bonnie. The officer assured us it was legal. We thanked her and headed on our way.

After the split, Joe continued to interject himself into my parents' lives. He'd stop by often, and he still called them Mom and Dad. I thought that was unusual; it seemed like he wanted to either annoy Sharon or keep tabs on her. I wondered then if it was because he hoped to eventually get her back, but he was also close to them. Joe's own father wasn't in the picture at all. I think his mother was really hard on him. I believe she eventually became dependent, and he helped care for her in the end. Joe moved her into his home.

I still worked as a manager at Radio Shack in the 1990s, back when cell phones were still a novel thing. I tried to convince Joe to get one. He didn't cave until just before his arrest.

"You know they can track you with those," Joe said.

Back then I thought, *Who cares if they track you?*

He also told me he didn't want his work—he spent three decades working for a grocery chain as a mechanic—to call him in for emergencies. Without a cell phone, they had to call his home phone and leave a message on the answering machine. He didn't typically answer no matter who was calling. He'd call back after you left a message.

I didn't think much of it then, but now I understand why he didn't want to risk being tracked.

Police came close to catching Joe nearly 20 years before his final arrest.

In 1996, Joe was arrested as part of a sting operation.

According to the *Sacramento Bee*, the operation targeted people who had outstanding warrants. They were told that they had won free Super Bowl tickets they could grab at a Sacramento office. Joe took the bait. He ended up in jail for a couple days on suspicion of holding up a gas station.

But they didn't take DNA samples. The technology existed, but it still hadn't caught on. There was nothing special about the arrest, according to the *Bee*, so police had no way of knowing they had just let the Golden State Killer go again.

Joe wasn't actually involved in a gas station hold up. He ended up suing the gas station for negligence and false imprisonment. The case was eventually settled and dismissed.[64]

I didn't know about this incident until this past year when I saw it on the news. Joe didn't mention it back then. It's strange to still be learning so much about someone I thought I knew.

My Wedding day Sept 15 1973 in Carmichael Ca.
Joe is second from the right.

Joe with my daughter in his lap about 1983.

Joe and his daughter visiting my daughters,
while Dad and I work on the spa deck, around 1984.

Joe comes over to look at the progress on a boat I built.
Around 1985 or '86

Joe admiring his radio control boat.

CHAPTER 14

A PUZZLING DISTANCE DEVELOPS

In the decade before the arrest, Joe put distance between us. Every now and then, I invited him to hang out. But he stopped taking me up on it and didn't return the invitation.

Around 2010, I invited Joe to join my nephew and me on my sailboat for a trip around the San Francisco Bay. The boat was a C & C Designs Newport 28, and I kept it berthed in the northern waterways that empty into the San Francisco Bay at Almar Marina in Martinez.

Usually when I'd sail her, we'd steer lazily north into the Suisun Point Channel at four or five knots for an afternoon ride. Sometimes we'd cruise right through San Pablo Bay into San Francisco Bay and moor up at the quiet city of Alameda in the East Bay. The boat moved slowly, so getting there would take half a day. I'd relax into the evening after the tie-up, sleep on the boat, and slip out into the misty waters of the next day's sunrise or when the tide was in my favor.

The first time I took Joe out on the boat, I took a video.

Joe was calm that day, and he seemed happy. We sailed by ships in the Navy's National Defense Reserve Fleet. It was calm and quiet that day as we glided past the impressive ships. I pointed out a particularly cool battle cruiser, and Joe said, "Can you imagine when it was in action and it was blastin' them frickin' guns and shit?"

I called Joe in 2010 to confirm another rendezvous, telling him our nephew, Matt, would be along for the ride, but he waved me off and said he didn't want to come. We'd always spent time together, so this seemed like a sudden change to me. Now I think he was making new friends who didn't know about his past life, friends who didn't know where he lived during which years. In 2007 he spent more time with people like Richard Mangang. Mangang worked with Joe at the Save Mart Distribution Center. They both loved to go fishing and they cultivated a friendship, going fishing at least once a week together.

"If you fish you have one thing in common," Mangang told the news outlet *Oxygen*. "I showed him how to fish with live bait, he showed me how to fish with lures."[65]

As Mangang described it in the interview, Joe gave him good advice on how to be a better man for his family. Joe went out of his way to be nice to people and do extra things to help out in his later years. He sometimes changed the oil in Nicole's car when she got to be old enough to drive and visit her cousin.

I saw him around 2014 when I bought a truck to tow a

trailer. He told me the motor in it would last forever but that I should replace the starter on it.

He was a purist. He wouldn't buy automatic cars; he'd only buy manuals. They were more reliable, he said.

He told me once about his favorite car, the Toyota Corolla sedan with a five-speed, one you can push to start. If the battery or starter went bad, it was a cheap, easy repair. He wasn't about to get stranded. Joe was all about reliability. He bought several Toyota Corollas over the years. He bought a brand-new one just a year or two before his arrest. Now I know there were underlying reasons why he wouldn't want something to stop working unexpectedly.

Last year in Carson City, Nevada, I had trouble starting my truck. I recalled what Joe had said years before, so I got a new starter and new batteries for the truck in the winter of 2018. I didn't want to get stranded either.

I sold my house and moved full time into an RV in June of 2016 to enjoy my retirement. The last time I saw Joe was right before I sold my house. Mom broke her hip after she took a fall in the garden and had to use a walker for about four months as part of her recovery. I came over to build a ramp for her with some wood I had lying around. I hadn't planned to see Joe, but he was there, checking in on Mom, too.

Apparently, she'd asked him to come over and install some disability bars in the bathroom. He was over at the house measuring the bathroom to get it all set up. I think I helped him finish the job. He seemed surprised to see me. For the last several years or so, he had kind of avoided me.

But that didn't stop him from coming by to help Mom. He had come by to help her in 2009, too, just after my dad passed. He had moved Dad's rifle outside, since my mother doesn't like guns and wanted it out of the house. Joe told her she could get some good money for it, so I took it to a gun shop for her to sell it. I think I got around $180 for it, which I gave to Mom.

The rifle I used to go rabbit hunting with Joe back in 1973 was missing. I don't know when it disappeared, but I discovered it was gone around 1998 when I moved. As with so many things now, I look back and wonder if Joe had anything to do with its disappearance. Was he covering his tracks somehow? Or did I just misplace an old gun I didn't use anymore?

I knew he'd lived in places where the Golden State Killer had shown up. I'd gone to visit him and Sharon a few times. But I didn't follow much of the news, and I hadn't read anything about it. I didn't see the FBI announcement in 2016 launching a campaign to catch the Golden State Killer, offering a $50,000 reward. I was in Idaho getting ready to visit Yellowstone then. Had I seen the news linking all the crimes together, I would have paid attention.

Would I have figured it out? It's impossible to say—but I wish I had.

Over the years, my relationship with Sharon changed,

too. We were the closest of my siblings growing up. My daughter, Deanna, even worked as a legal secretary for Sharon's law firm for several years. Deanna eventually found Mr. Right and got married. After that, she didn't need to work anymore and wanted to be a stay-at-home mom. She gave notice and trained a replacement, then quit. Sharon didn't take well to that. I disagreed with how Sharon handled the situation, and our relationship has been a bit distant since.

Though I lost touch with Joe toward the end, he seemed to be working to make nice and make new friends. Like me, many of those new friends were shocked by the news that they, too, knew one of the most prolific alleged serial killers the nation's ever seen.

Joe retired from Save Mart Distribution Center just before the arrest.

Gary Griffin, a coworker and neighbor, told news outlets that Joe seemed like a normal guy. Griffin ate lunch with him every day for decades and even went waterskiing with him. Other coworkers remembered him as being a meticulous mechanic who never called in sick to work.[66]

The day after Joe was arrested, a *New York Post* article repeated his neighbor's comments that Joe often "did good deeds for his neighbors," including building a new fence for one.

"You would have thought something like that would show in his eyes," Griffin told a reporter.

Joe's coworker Richard Mangang told interviewers,

"Damn, I've known this guy all this time, and I would have never guessed. The guy I knew was a nice guy!"

Another neighbor, Jim Chappell, said, "He was always friendly to all the neighbors. … We called him the yeller, but come to find out he was a little hard of hearing."[67]

For more than 40 years, Joe evaded capture.

Ray Biondie, a retired detective with the Sacramento County Sheriff's Department called the Golden State Killer one of the most prolific criminals out there in a 2016 plea to the public for information. In that same plea to the public, Sgt. Paul Belli said the Golden State Killer "isn't concerned about human life. He enjoys the terror. He enjoys inflicting that type of emotional pain on people."

Even in 2016, the FBI had DNA samples taken from victims. They just didn't have a suspect to match.

Detective Paul Holes helped spearhead efforts to finally put all the pieces together. His work on the case began 24 years ago, when he worked as an investigator with the Contra Costa County Sheriff's Office. After hitting a dead end with criminal DNA databases, he ran the samples through GEDmatch, a public genealogy site. Most people using the site send in their DNA to learn more about where they came from or to find family members.[68]

Using the site, Holes was able to find some 20 matches linking to distant relatives somewhere in the ranks of third cousins. That got him closer than he'd been before, turning up a great-great-great grandparent, according to the *Washington Post*. From there, he built out family trees using newspapers, census data, and a gravesite locator. Then he narrowed down the list to men who would have been around the right age with the right connections to California.

Holes himself was set to retire in March 2018, after spending more than two decades on the Golden State Killer case. Nevertheless, the day before he was set to be done with it all, he was staking out Joe's home.

It wasn't his first time working to get male DNA samples to see if any would come up as possible matches for the DNA profiles he ran through the GEDmatch program. He'd knocked on many doors and spoken with countless men over the course of his career asking for DNA samples. He had a shtick. He'd apologize for the interruption, explain who he was, and tell them that their name had come up during an investigation. People usually complied, and it wasn't a big deal. Most of the time, Holes ruled them out and never encountered them again.

But he opted not to confront Joe; instead, he collected a couple of DNA samples.

According to the arrest warrant, law enforcement collected DNA from the driver's side car door handle on April 20, 2018. At the time, the car was parked outside the Hobby Lobby store in Roseville. The samples were collected while Joe shopped inside the store, unaware of how close he was to being caught after all those years.

DNA experts at the Sacramento DA Crime Lab compared the DNA to one of the Orange County profiles collected from the murders of Lyman and Charlene Smith in 1980. It was identical, according to the arrest warrant.[69]

DNA tests use genetic markers to find similarities and differences in different DNA samples. Tests typically use at least a dozen markers. Tests that use more markers are usually more accurate, though it drives up the cost. According to a report by *National Geographic*, the probability of the DNA profiles of two unrelated people matching is, on average, less than one in one billion.

On April 23, 2018, more samples were collected from Joe's trash can outside his house. Law enforcement officials watched as he put the trash out on the street the night before.

A simple piece of tissue, encoded with a healthy dose of Joe's DNA, offered the break detectives chased for more than 40 years. It, too, matched the profile built from the Orange County and Ventura County crimes.

The results came back a perfect match, and Joe was arrested. Though there hasn't been a trial yet, and Joe is innocent until proven guilty in a court of law, law enforcement is confident about the match.

There's been endless speculation about why Joe did what he did. Holes told media outlets before the arrest that it seemed like a retaliatory attack, as victims reported their attacker saying things like, "I hate you, Bonnie."

"Most certainly if he's making the statement, 'I hate you, Bonnie,' while he's attacking another female, he is what we call an anger retaliatory rapist," Holes told the *Mercury News*. "I do believe that's what happened here. I don't know what made him that way, but you've got to think Bonnie dumped him, he's not happy about that, he still has feelings for her, who knows? But something along those lines must have happened."[70]

Jesse Ryland, one of Joe's nephews, told *BuzzFeed News* that Joe was playing with his sister, Constance, in an abandoned warehouse on base when Joe was around nine or 10 years old and Constance was around seven. Two airmen, according to Ryland, walked in and raped her in front of Joe.

"That's pretty crazy for a kid to see his sister be violated," Ryland, 35, told *BuzzFeed*. "Maybe that was the start of Joe going wacko."

According to the report, Ryland learned about the rape from Constance, his mother, right before she died from cancer in 2017.[71]

But we'll never really know what he was thinking unless he says something publicly or a psychiatric evaluation gets released to the public.

CHAPTER 15

OUR FAMILY AFTER THE ARREST

After the arrest, life felt surreal. Reporters hounded our family.

The FBI tore through Joe's house looking for evidence after the arrest. When they were finished, the inside of the house was torn up. They left holes in the walls and pulled up the carpet. Misha, who lived there at the time, was left to clean up the mess.

Nicole went over to help her. At that point, it had been years since she had last seen Joe. She was busy with her three children, but she went, not wanting Misha to face the task of picking up all the pieces alone.

Among the wreckage, Nicole spotted an invitation she had sent Joe asking him to attend her son Jackson's first birthday party the previous year. Jackson's little face smiled up at her in the picture, surrounded by balloons. Joe didn't go to the party—he wasn't one to enjoy big social gatherings. But he had kept the invitation.

In the immediate aftermath, people threw toilet paper,

eggs, and dog poop at the house. Misha had to get a security camera and a lock box to help keep the place safe. She eventually moved out and planned to sell the house.

About two weeks after the arrest, Tessa, Joe's youngest daughter, called to tell me she had gotten engaged and was planning to get married in Hawaii in October. She invited me out to a fancy dinner to celebrate. I was still in town, so I decided to go. Tessa's fiancé's parents were there, and so were a couple of her best friends. Sharon was there, too. I was surprised; they'd all just been through a pretty traumatic couple of weeks.

Joe was the elephant in the room. No one talked about it. Everybody knew, but no one wanted to bring up such a negative thing to ruin the moment.

I got the feeling Sharon wanted to reconnect after we'd lost touch. I ended up staying in the area for about two months after the news.

Nicole said the whole thing has affected her more than she wants to admit. Joe was her uncle. They were very close, and she remembers her childhood as one filled with happy memories.

Nicole can only think of Joe one way, not as the monster he has been depicted as.

So far, I have remained under the radar and tell few people I meet camping about who I am or what happened. When I do tell people, the reactions range from not even knowing about the Golden State Killer to just having heard something about him and the crimes. Most want to know when the book is coming out and are looking forward to reading it.

CHAPTER 16

SERIAL KILLER SIMILARITIES ARE CLUES

The existence of serial killers is not new. Accounts of those kinds of horrific crimes are well documented throughout history around the world, according to the FBI. In 1886, for example, Richard Von Krafft-Ebing first published his textbook *Psychopathia Sexualis.* In it, he detailed case studies of sexual homicide, serial murder, and other crimes.

It's still a rare thing, making up less than 1% of murders each year, according to the FBI. But such crimes do capture the public's attention, and in the 1970s and 80s, real monsters prowled the streets. In the Sacramento area alone, at least two other serial killers were active around the same time as Joe allegedly was.[72]

VAMPIRE OF SACRAMENTO

One such monster, Richard Trenton Chase, was known as the Vampire of Sacramento. Chase cannibalized and drank the blood of six people.

In 1977, Chase shot and killed Ambrose Griffin as he stood unloading groceries in his driveway. Chase sped away right after.

Chase killed five of his victims between January 23, 1978, and January 27, 1978. They'd been shot and extensively slashed, according to the *Napa Valley Register* archives. Among the victims was a pregnant woman and two children.

Sacramento County Sheriff Duane Lowe said at the time that those murders were the most grotesque slayings he'd seen in his 28 years of police work, according to *Napa Valley Register* archives. Chase was arrested January 28, 1978. At the time of the arrest, he was holding a large cardboard box containing bloody rags and a .22-caliber gun.

The Radford University database provides information on serial killers and was developed by Mike Aamodt, professor emeritus at Radford University. According to the database, Chase began killing and torturing animals, including cats, when he was around 10 years old. He had family troubles, too. His mother saw two psychiatrists, and his family eventually lost their house. Chase got Cs, Ds, and Fs while he attended Mira Loma High School. I'm sure the heavy weed habit he picked up his sophomore year of high school didn't help him in the grades department.

When Chase was 18, he saw a psychiatrist because of erectile dysfunction, according to the Radford database. His psychiatrist told him then his problem might be caused by suppressed anger and mental illness, but Chase didn't get any further counseling.[73]

In the spring of 1971, he enrolled in American River College, a part of Joe's hunting grounds.

In November 1972, Chase's parents finalized their divorce. He went on a trip to Utah by himself and was put in jail for a traffic violation.

By April 1973, his behavior had started to escalate. While at a friend's apartment party, Chase fondled a girl and was asked to leave, according to the database. He left but then returned. Cops were called to escort him out. As they did, a .22-caliber gun fell from his belt. He spent some time in jail before his father bailed him out.

In December 1973, Chase told doctors at the American River Hospital someone stole his pulmonary artery and that his blood flow had stopped. He was admitted to the psychiatric ward, but his mother took him out. He spent time in and out of the hospital for a few years after that.

On April 26, 1976, Chase's father found him in his apartment. He was extremely sick, according to the Radford database. Chase said his blood was poisoned after he'd injected himself with rabbit's blood.

He was transferred to an extended-care mental hospital in May 1976. He apparently believed he was there for a bad case of food poisoning. Housekeepers at the place noted they regularly found dead birds outside his room. He later told a psychiatrist he believed his own blood was poisoned, according to the *Register*. Chase got out of the hospital once his court-ordered conservatorship expired.

In August 1977, police officers with the Bureau of Indian Affairs found Chase near the Pyramid Lake Reservation in Nevada. He'd killed a cow, taken out its liver, and smeared its blood all over his naked body.

Chase then took the body of his youngest victim, David Ferreira, 22 months, with him after a January 27 murder spree. A city-wide search launched to find David.

On January 28, 1978, police knocked on Chase's door, and when he came out, police tackled him and took him into custody. Police finally found David's body in a cardboard box in a vacant lot between a church and a supermarket on March 24, 1978, according to the Radford archive.

According to the *Los Angeles Times* archives, Chase began rambling about UFOs, Nazis, the FBI, and the CIA during his trial. Despite some indications that he wasn't fully lucid, the jury rejected his plea of not guilty by reason of insanity and found him guilty of murder. He died while on death row after overdosing on antidepressants.

BEDROOM BASHER

An attacker dubbed the Bedroom Basher also made headlines in the Sacramento area between 1978 and 1979, while Joe was allegedly active.

The attacker was known to knock his victims unconscious with blunt objects, according to the *Los Angeles Times* archives, and then rape or attempt to rape them. At the time, the attacks were dubbed one of the most notorious serial-killing sprees in the county's history, with the Basher killing five women and one unborn child.[74]

Kevin Lee Green was convicted of six counts of murder in 1980. He was married to Dianna Green, one of the victims. Dianna was bludgeoned but not killed, though the attack resulted in the death of her unborn baby. The attack left Dianna herself brain damaged.

Green claimed he was innocent, but a jury found him guilty and he spent 16 years in prison. However, in 1996, DNA samples exonerated Green. Law enforcement discovered DNA samples collected at the scene of the attack instead matched with a man named Gerald Parker.

At the time, Parker was serving time in Corcoran Prison for violating his parole.

According to the *San Bernardino County Sun* archives, detectives confronted Parker with the new evidence. While the specifics of the conversation weren't revealed, police said the interview led to the new charges.

Parker had raped and bludgeoned to death five women between the ages of 17 and 31, according to *Tulare Advance-Register* archives. He had attacked women in the Orange County towns of Anaheim, Costa Mesa, and Tustin. Parker lived in Orange County at the time and was stationed as a Marine staff sergeant.[75]

Despite the new evidence, Green's ex-wife still believed Green beat and raped her. She even testified against him. She had temporary memory loss after she emerged from a coma after the attack, but she said memories of the attack came back to her while she was reading a baby magazine. She said she remembered Green being the one to attack her.

They'd argued that night. She said Green raped her when she refused to have sex with him. He said he had left the house after their argument to get a hamburger and calm down. Green's attorneys argued that Dianna's memory couldn't be trusted, but the jury believed her at the time, according to the *Register*.

Dianna later visited Parker in prison and asked him what he remembered. Parker told her, according to the *Register*, that he had watched the couple in their home from his van as he drank and used drugs. He watched Green leave. Parker said he then went into the house and found Dianna unconscious, and proceeded to hit and rape her.

In 2017, the California Supreme Court upheld Parker's death sentence, according to the *Orange County Register*.[76]

TED BUNDY

Ted Bundy is largely regarded as one of America's most prolific serial killers. Though he was executed three decades ago, his name remains at the forefront of the country's consciousness. He was convicted for killing at least 30 people, though the actual number of victims could be much higher. He roamed Colorado, Florida, Oregon, and Washington killing young women between 1974 and 1978. One of his first known crimes took place in February 1974, when he abducted and strangled Lynda Ann Healy near the University of Washington.

Bundy often pretended to be injured to lure young women to his aid. He kept crutches, slings, and plaster for casts at home, so he could dress himself up. He'd pretend to need help loading stuff into his car while his young prey kindly offered to give him a hand. Then he'd strike.

He killed at least 11 people in 1974. In 1975, he killed at least six people before he was arrested for the first time. Highway patrol pulled him over in Granger, Utah. Police found suspicious items in his car, such as gloves, rope, and handcuffs. A woman he once tried to abduct later identified him in a lineup. He was charged with aggravated kidnapping and attempted criminal assault and was found guilty. Despite being locked up, his crimes didn't end there.

In 1976, Bundy was charged with the murder of Caryn Campbell. He pleaded not guilty and went on to work on his own defense.

Because Bundy was working on the case, he had access to the Pitkin County jailhouse law library. He escaped through a window about 25 feet above the ground, hightailing it to the mountains in Aspen. Police picked him up about five days later, but that still wasn't the end.

In 1977, Bundy managed to escape once again. This time, he climbed through an opening in the ceiling made for a light fixture. He went on to kill at least three more people before police caught him for a final time.

In 1978, he killed Margaret Bowman and Lisa Levy, two Florida State University students. The women were found bludgeoned to death in their sorority house. Bundy left a deep bite mark on Levy's left buttock, one of his signature moves.

Kimberly Leach was his last known victim. She was 12 years old. She disappeared in the middle of a school day. Her body was eventually found near Suwannee River State Park.

On January 24, 1989, Bundy was executed via electric chair.

Despite the horrific crimes he committed, Bundy had a long-time girlfriend. Elizabeth Kloepfer thought he was a normal guy for much of their relationship. Kloepfer had met Bundy just before he killed his first victim. She was young, recently divorced, and had a young daughter. She thought she had met a man who could step up and be a father for her daughter.

They were in an on-again-off-again relationship for about seven years. For a long time, she didn't know about his crimes, but she did eventually come to suspect him and reported Bundy to police. A movie depicting her relationship with

Bundy came out in 2019 called *Extremely Wicked, Shockingly Evil and Vile.*

In a not-so-normal turn of events, Bundy got married—not to Kloepfer, but to a woman named Carole Ann Boone. The two first met in 1974. At the time, they both worked for the Washington State Department of Emergency Services, according to *The Only Living Witness: The True Story of Serial Sex Killer Ted Bundy.* He would have been with Kloepfer at the time.

Boone and Bundy developed a friendship that eventually culminated into something more. According to *Rolling Stone* magazine, some think she gave Bundy money to help him when he escaped prison in 1977. While Bundy was on trial, he and Boone got married. In 1982, they had a child together. Boone divorced Bundy before he was executed.

Bundy's story is heartbreaking, wild, and weird, but I noticed a handful of traits that he and Joe had in common.

As a teen, Bundy was known to be a Peeping Tom. He also had a habit of shoplifting.

According to an A&E interview with Al Carlisle, a psychologist who interviewed Bundy, he also fell in love with a girl when he was young. When she ended it, Bundy couldn't let it go. It reminds me of how Joe felt about Bonnie.

Bundy's first girlfriend was a woman named Diane Edwards. She came from an affluent family; Bundy did not. She broke up with him when she sensed he didn't really have a plan for his life, according to Ann Rule, author of *The Stranger Beside Me*, a true crime story of Ted Bundy.

Edwards found Bundy to be "emotional and unsure of himself," according to the book. She also suspected he used people and took advantage of them. Those words stick out to me as I remember how Sharon described Joe as manipulative. Bundy thought the breakup was all about the money. He plotted an elaborate revenge for Edwards.

He sought to make something of himself, to become someone a high-class girl like Edwards wouldn't ignore. He re-enrolled in college, got involved with politics, rubbed shoulders with important people, and got accepted to law school.

In 1973, while he was dating Kloepfer, he set Edwards up. He reached out to rekindle the flame, convincing her that he was interested in marrying her. In 1974, he rejected her, like she'd rejected him, according to Rule.

Soon after, he began his murderous rampage.

Bundy also had an unusual childhood. In his early years, he grew up believing his mother was his sister. For a long time, his grandparents raised him like they were his parents.

Bundy's mother, Eleanor Louise Cowell, gave birth to him in 1946 at the Elizabeth Lund Home for Unwed Mothers in Burlington, Vermont. Cowell told people she'd been seduced by a sailor, but records show Bundy's father was an Air Force veteran named Lloyd Marshall. Over the years, many have speculated that Bundy's grandfather was his actual biological father in a case of incest, despite Cowell's denials.

By many accounts, Bundy adored his grandfather, even though the man was known to kick dogs and swing cats by their tails. Sometimes he'd even beat people who pissed him off. A psychiatrist who spoke to Bundy before his execution, Dorothy Otnow Lewis, noted Bundy's grandfather was an "extremely violent and frightening individual." She diagnosed Bundy with a manic-depressive disorder. She speculated the disorder originated early in Bundy's childhood while he lived in Philadelphia, according to the *Los Angeles Times* archives.[77]

When Bundy was about four years old, his mother moved with him to Washington State, where she married a man named Johnny Bundy. Bundy struggled to fit in. He had a speech impediment when he was young and grew more resentful of his parents when he learned Johnny wasn't his father.

"He got addicted to the idea of this possession of the essence of the victim," Carlisle said during his interview with A&E. "Bundy created himself through poor choices."

GREEN RIVER KILLER

Gary Ridgway, dubbed the Green River Killer, was arrested in 2001. He ended up pleading guilty to killing 49 women, though he later claimed to have killed around 80. He was known for picking up prostitutes, runaways, and drug addicts during the 1980s and 1990s in Washington. He, like Joe, was arrested with the help of advances in DNA technology.

He first killed, as far as we know, in 1982 near Seattle. His first victim was just 16 years old and had been living in a foster home. Ridgway strangled her to death. He was known to rape and murder women before throwing their bodies into or near the Green River in Washington.

Many parts of Ridgway's life seemed normal. He had a job painting trucks. He was married a couple of times, had a son, and served in the military. Like Joe, many of his neighbors thought he was a good guy.

According to an interview with the *News Tribune*, Ridgway's son, Matthew, remembered him as being a man who never yelled.[78] Ridgway took him camping in Washington and Oregon on alternating weekends after divorcing Matthew's mother. Ridgway even taught his son how to play baseball near the Green River. Matthew remembered his father always showed up for school concerts and soccer practices.

But Ridgway was a murderer fixated on having sex with dead bodies. He admitted to police he would give prostitutes a false sense of security by showing them his son's bedroom or his picture when he lured them into his house.

None of his three wives suspected what he did.

Katherine Ramsland, a forensic psychology and criminal justice professor at DeSales University in Pennsylvania, gave an interview to A&E.

"Successful serial killers with families are able to hide by partitioning their lives and protecting their secrets," Ramsland said. "As long as they have families that accept their 'normal' persona and don't probe too deeply, they can usually arrange their lives to have the time to kill."

Ramsland said Ridgway was too smart to kill his wives. He knew he would have been the lead suspect.

That's exactly what Joe did with us. He hid his true nature. We all accepted it as Joe being Joe. The little red flags never added up enough. He hid in plain sight the whole time. In some sense, I'm glad I'm not the only person who's ever missed the signs of evil. It seems so impossible that we didn't see it—but so many others hadn't either.

In a weird twist of events, police had Ted Bundy consult on the Green River Killer investigation while he was in prison in Florida. His consult paid off. Bundy told police the killer's new disposal site was probably closer to his home, according to *Oxygen*. Police made a triangle around the area, and, sure enough, Ridgway's home was in the red zone.

JOHN WAYNE GACY

Between 1972 and 1978, John Wayne Gacy murdered at least 33 teenage boys and young men in the Chicago area. He was known to either pretend he was a police officer or offer to pay for sex to convince his young victims to come close.

Sometimes he'd just offer younger men weed and beer, and they'd come over to his house. When he got them alone, he'd rape and torture his victims before he strangled them. Then he'd bury them in the crawl space under his house.

Gacy seemed like a mostly normal guy when he wasn't raping and murdering people. He got married in 1964 and had two children. He worked for his father-in-law then.

Gacy got in trouble with the law before he became a murderer. In 1968, he was arrested for sexually assaulting two teenage boys. He was convicted and sentenced to a decade in prison, though he got out in just 18 months. His wife divorced him in the aftermath.

He remarried, ran a contracting business, dabbled in politics, and hosted dinner parties. He even volunteered at children's charity events, often dressing up as "Patches" or "Pogo the Clown," according to *Oxygen*. This earned him the moniker "The Killer Clown." Though there's no evidence he ever killed anyone while he was in costume, the name and the imagery stuck.

Gacy was caught when he deviated from his normal selection of runaways and vulnerable men. His last victim was well-known in the community.

Gacy was found guilty and sentenced to death. During the 14 years he spent on death row, Gacy spent plenty of time selling creepy clown paintings to collectors. He painted a clown with a white face, giant blue patches over the eyes, and sharp, triangular eyebrows; the painted red lips curved up into a sharp smile.

According to the *Chicago Tribune*, Gacy's crimes drove law enforcement to make some significant strides. Back then, law enforcement agencies worked largely on their own. It took a long time to connect all the pieces of the case, because federal and local law enforcement didn't communicate well with each other at that time. Gacy's case changed some of that. Agencies started sharing information on runaways and sex offenders with each other. They also established a national hotline and created a computer database for missing people.[79]

CHAPTER 17

MYTHS ABOUT SERIAL KILLERS

Myths about serial killers persist in the public conscience. Individual stories tend to get dramatized and sensationalized. I wanted to learn the truth, so I dug into FBI documents to learn more about the truth behind serial killers.

MYTH: SERIAL KILLERS ARE LONERS AND WEIRDOS

According to the FBI, most serial killers appear quite normal. They hide in plain sight, just like Joe. They often have steady jobs, families, homes, and friends.

Robert Yates, a decorated US Army National Guard helicopter pilot, enjoyed a middle-class lifestyle around Spokane, Washington. Yet he murdered at least 16 people, possibly 18 or more. His oldest known victim was 47, and his youngest was 16. His crimes made headlines in the 1990s as he gunned women down. He often targeted prostitutes and had sex with their dead bodies.

Once, he even buried a woman's body in his backyard, underneath his bedroom window. He went so far as to plant flowers over the corpse. He later told police where they could find her body in hopes of avoiding the death penalty.

Like Joe, Yates was known for most of his life as a normal family man. When he was arrested for his crimes, he'd been married to his wife for nearly 30 years and had five kids. Despite how active Yates was, his family didn't suspect anything. Much like we were, they were caught off guard.

According to a report by the Associated Press, his wife, Linda, caught him burning credit card statements in the fireplace in 1999. She dug deeper, learning the card had charges for a place called Al's Spa Tub Motel; customers could pay by the hour there, but she'd never been there with him. Linda thought she had caught her husband cheating on her. She didn't know he was a serial killer.

Like Joe, Yates had a brief relationship with a woman before he settled down with Linda. Yates had married a woman named Shirley Nylander when he was 20. They separated after about 18 months.

Yates married Linda before his divorce was finalized, and they had their first child shortly after. Less than a year later, Yates killed his first victims—a young couple—in 1975. He shot them while they were on a picnic.

MYTH: SERIAL KILLERS ARE GENIUSES OR INSANE

Another myth, according to the FBI, is that all serial killers are either insane or are evil geniuses. Many have speculated that

Joe must have been some kind of genius to evade law enforcement for so long.

Now that I know Joe is the prime suspect, some of those words seem crazy to me. I never thought of Joe as particularly smart. Honestly, I was surprised to learn he got top grades in college. It always seemed to take him a long time to grasp concepts that came quickly to others. It took him a while to wrap his mind around things.

I also never noticed anything in Joe's behavior that would have led me to believe he was insane—odd maybe, but not insane. Obviously, normal people don't go about committing heinous acts of violence, so something else has to be going on if they aren't all diagnosed as insane.

However, serial killers do have higher tendencies to developing personality disorders such as psychopathy, personality disorder, and others, according to the FBI. Also, they range in having borderline to above-average intelligence levels, which is about the same as the rest of the population.

MYTH: THEY CAN'T STOP KILLING PEOPLE

The media largely speculated that the Golden State Killer was dead or already in prison because the murders stopped in 1986.

According to the FBI, several serial killers out there have stopped killing before they got caught. There are a number of reasons why someone might stop committing crimes. It could be they got too old to engage in such physical activity. It could be they got more involved with their families or found some other sexual substitution or other diversions, according to the FBI.

As far as we know, Joe allegedly stopped raping and murdering people after he had two kids. He got a new job as a truck mechanic around 1988. I can't speak to any other kind of sexual diversions, but Joe was busy with the family, often helping to watch my own kids.

Dennis Rader, also known as "Bind, Torture, Kill," or "BTK," murdered 10 people between 1974 and 1991 in Wichita, Kansas. He stopped after that.

He had a reputation for taunting police, local media, and the community at large. Sometimes he'd make phone calls or send letters, hoping BTK would get credit for the crimes. According to *Oxygen*, Rader once explained to police in a letter that he had gotten a taste for brutal, sexual murders when he watched porn as a boy. He developed violent fantasies as a teen. He later got into window-peeping and stealing women's underwear.

As an adult, Rader was married and had two children. His daughter, Kerri Rawson, recently spoke to *20/20* about the case and how it impacted her family.

"If we had had an inkling that my father had harmed anyone, let anyone murdered anyone, let alone 10, we would've gone screaming out that door to the police station," she told *20/20*. "We were living our normal life. We looked like a normal American family because we were a normal family. And then everything upended on us."

Rawson still writes to her father. She still loves him, even though she recognizes he did horrific things, she told *20/20*.

I don't blame her.

Joe's daughters still think of him as Dad. They still love him. Like Rawson, they remember their dad as a good man and a loving father.

Maybe Rader, like Joe, got so busy with raising a family he no longer had time to terrorize the city.

According the FBI, Rader substituted his murderous interests with "autoerotic activities," which involved his cutting off his own oxygen supply to heighten his sexual experience. At this stage, he'd often take selfies dressed in women's clothes. He wore masks and bound himself, too. Sometimes he even took pictures of himself wearing his victims' clothes.

Rader stopped killing people in 1991. He was caught in 2005.

Jeffery Gorton killed his first victim in 1986 and his next in 1991, according to the FBI. He stopped killing after that, choosing instead to get involved with cross-dressing and masturbating, as well as normal consensual sex with his wife. Gorton was caught in 2002.

MYTH: ALL SERIAL KILLERS ARE MOTIVATED ONLY BY SEX

According to the FBI, serial murderers can be motivated by many other things, including anger, thrill, financial gain, and attention-seeking.

John Allen Muhammad, a former US Army Staff Sergeant, and his accomplice Lee Boyd Malvo were motivated by anger and thrill-seeking, according to the FBI. The two worked as serial snipers, terrorizing Washington, DC, for three weeks. They shot 13 people, killing 10.

Among their victims was a woman who worked as an FBI analyst, shot as she ran errands with her husband at The Home Depot. Another woman was killed while she vacuumed out her van at a gas station in Maryland. Another victim was a middle school boy heading to class.

Muhammad was executed in 2009.

Like Joe, they had communicated with police. But whereas Joe taunted law enforcement, Muhammad and Malvo tried to extort money to stop the shootings.

According to a report by the *Los Angeles Times*, a clearer motive did emerge following interviews with Malvo conducted by mental health experts.

Malvo was 17 at the time of the shootings. The shootings, he told interviewers, were part of a mission to incite racial revolution in response to oppression, with the ultimate goal of setting up a utopian black colony in Canada focused on racial and social justice. According to Malvo's defense attorneys, he was essentially brainwashed by Muhammad.

Another case is Michael Swango, a former US Marine, ambulance worker, and physician. According to the FBI, he was convicted of four murders in Ohio and New York, but authorities suspect he killed between 35 and 50 people across the United States and Africa using poison. Authorities never nailed down a motive. Swango kept a scrap book with various newspaper and magazine clippings about natural disasters.

The FBI pointed to another case involving a man named Paul Reid. Reid robbed a couple of fast food restaurants in Tennessee. He'd gain control of the situation, then either stab or shoot his victims. Over the course of his crime spree, he killed at least seven people. The FBI identified his primary motive to be getting rid of the witnesses of the robberies. He used the cash he grabbed to buy a car.

MYTH: ALL SERIAL KILLERS TRAVEL TO KILL, ESPECIALLY INTERSTATE

According to the FBI, most serial killers have a very defined geographic area in which they operate. They kill where they feel comfortable—near their home, their work, or relatives' homes.

For years, it appeared the Golden State Killer was traveling across California to kill. It turns out, those travels aligned with where Joe and Sharon lived at the time.

According to the FBI, some serial killers do step outside their comfort zones when they feel particularly confident about their level of experience and ability to avoid getting caught. Most who travel, according to the FBI, do so because they move from place to place, like Joe; are homeless and transient; or travel a lot for work, such as truck drivers or those in military service.

MYTH: SERIAL KILLERS WANT TO GET CAUGHT

The Golden State Killer was known to call police and victims alike to taunt them before and after he committed crimes. He also had a signature style law enforcement came to recognize. Yet that didn't necessarily mean he wanted to get caught.

According to the FBI, serial killers often plan out their crimes more thoroughly than other criminals, but the learning curve is steep. They must "select, target, approach, control, and dispose of their victims," according to an FBI report on serial murder.

As they continue to commit crimes without getting caught, serial killers can get cocky. They start to feel like they can't get caught, so they take more risks—eventually leading to their capture.

MYTH: ALL SERIAL KILLERS ARE WHITE MEN

While many high-profile killers are white men, that's not the full story. Serial killers span all racial groups and genders, according to the FBI, mirroring the general population.

Charles Ng

Charles Ng was a Hong Kong native and former US Marine. He was discharged after he was caught stealing, much like Joe. Though, unlike Joe, Ng served time for it. He ended up serving about three years for attempting to steal weapons.

In 1999, Ng was convicted of killing 11 people, including two toddlers at a cabin, according to the *Los Angeles Times* archives. However, some estimate Ng and his friend, Leonard Lake, also a former Marine, killed about 35 people—including Lake's own brother.

Lake served two tours in the Vietnam War as a radar operator. He was discharged in 1971. As a child, Lake took naked pictures of his sisters and allegedly extorted them for sexual favors.

The two worked together to kidnap victims and take their money. They stole their victims' identities, collecting checks and selling off their stuff.

Ng and Lake used women as sex slaves before murdering them, according to the *Times*. The two kept the women in a cinder-block bunker, lined with a one-way mirror so they could keep watch. The room the women were forced to stay in had three things inside: a bucket, toilet paper, and a list of rules. One of the posted rules read, "I must always be ready to service my master. I must be clean, brushed, and made-up with my cell neat."

Ng's sticky fingers got them caught in 1985.

Ng and Lake went to a hardware store near the cabin bunker to replace a vice they used on their victims. Ng was spotted shoplifting, and witnesses called police. He ran, but police caught Lake. He had an illegal firearm on him.

While in custody, Lake managed to swallow two cyanide pills. He died not long after. Ng escaped to Canada for about a week before he shoplifted again. He shot a security guard, but he was apprehended by law enforcement. Eventually he was extradited to the US.

Ng's father, Kenneth, testified in 1999 in an effort to save Ng from the death penalty.

According to the *Los Angeles Times* archives, Kenneth told the court in "halting English" that he severely beat Ng as a child, sometimes tethering him and whipping him with a stick.

"I tried to bring him up the right way," Kenneth testified. "Unfortunately, I [used] the wrong way. I [thought] this [was] normal. But now I know how wrong I am."

In 1999, Ng was sentenced to death, though thanks to a moratorium on the death penalty, Ng is still alive and serving time in San Quentin, a prison in California.

Derrick Todd Lee

Derrick Todd Lee, an African-American man, was convicted of killing two women. He was suspected of killing seven women in Baton Rouge, Louisiana, between 1992 and 2003. He was sentenced to death, but died of cardiovascular disease in 2016, according to the *Daily Advertiser*.

Lee graduated from West Feliciana High School, where he played the snare drum in the school band. He took vocational courses as a special-education student, according to the *Post*. He got married and had two kids, but had a reputation for chasing women, whether it was wanted or not.

He was known for being a Peeping Tom, even in his early teen years, according to the *Advocate*. He wasn't arrested for it as a minor, but he was as an adult.

Like Joe, burglary was also among the crimes Lee committed. He was arrested and convicted of burglary in 1992, earning a two-year sentence before law enforcement caught on to his more serious crimes.

Coral Eugene Watts

Coral Eugene Watts, an African American man, killed five people in Michigan before he fled to Texas. He killed another 12 people before authorities caught him. According to the *New York Times*, Watts was a suspect in 26 other slayings, and he might have killed more than 80 women. His crime spree ran from about 1974 to 1982.

Watts had a history of issues. When he was 15, he attacked a woman on his paper route, according to *CBS News*. He spent years drifting in and out of psychiatric hospitals.

Police suspected that he was involved in murders in Detroit, but there wasn't enough evidence to arrest him. In 1980, his crimes gained more notoriety as media and law enforcement began calling him the "Sunday Morning Slasher." Authorities believed Watts killed women randomly. He drowned, stabbed, hanged, and strangled his victims.

He confessed to 12 murders in 1982 in a deal with Texas prosecutors. That deal almost allowed him to go free after serving just 24 years of his 60-year sentence. However, he was tried for the 1974 murder of a Western Michigan University student and got a life sentence that time around. Watts died in Foote Hospital of prostate cancer in 2007.

Juan Corona

Juan Corona, a Mexican man living in Yuba City, California, killed 25 migrant farmworkers in 1971. He was caught when a farmer in Sutter County found a freshly dug hole in a peach orchard, according to the *Los Angeles Times*. The next day, the farmer found the hole filled with dirt. Suspicious, he called sheriff's deputies.

Deputies found a man's body in the shallow grave May 19, 1971.

His head had been hacked off, according to the *Times*, and he had suffered many stab wounds.[80]

As investigators searched, they found more bodies. Armed with picks and shovels, deputies probed the earth around Feather River for more graves, according to the *San Francisco Examiner* archives. Corona was arrested around 4:30 a.m. May 26, 1971, in his Yuba City home. He didn't resist arrest.[81]

Many of Corona's victims were farmworkers, buried in shallow graves along the Feather River, which is north of Sacramento. Most of his victims had been stabbed with a machete. One was shot.

Corona was known as a quiet man. Many people knew him, but no one knew him well, according to the *San Bernardino County Sun* archives. Corona was married to a woman named Gloria, his second wife. They had four children together. In an interview with the *Sun*, she said he "always treated me right and was never violent with me or our four children."

Most of the people the paper interviewed said Corona was a quiet, good man who didn't ruffle feathers. But a couple people said they feared him, especially after a violent incident involving Corona's oldest brother around February 25, 1970.

A farmworker was found in the restroom of a cantina one morning, viciously beaten with wounds on the back of his head, like the bodies of the men found along the Feather River. The man survived but was badly disfigured. According to the *Sun*, he needed plastic surgery.

According to the *Los Angeles Times*, the motive around the killings remained a mystery until Corona's death in 2019. Corona struggled with mental illness. He was admitted twice into a state mental hospital in Auburn, where he received a diagnosis of schizophrenia.

Police determined the first murder happened around April 1, 1971, and the last occurred May 19, 1971, when the first body was discovered, according to the *Lompoc Record* archives. Investigators found copies of receipts with Juan Corona's name in one of the graves.[82]

The company I worked for at the time was hired to take some aerial photographs of the shallow grave sites after Corona was captured. I was the photographer. I took the photos and was later questioned by the District Attorney's office. They wanted to know how detailed the maps were regarding the location of the burial sites.

In 1973, a jury found him guilty and he was sentenced to 25 consecutive life terms.

But things got a little weird. A state appellate court overturned the first conviction, calling out Corona's defense for not bringing up a single witness when the prosecution had brought up 119 witnesses.

The second time around, Corona's defense attorney tried to shift blame onto Corona's late older brother. The jury still found him guilty. He died in prison at the age of 85.

Rafael Resendez-Ramirez

Rafael Resendez-Ramirez, a Mexico native, killed at least nine people in three states before he turned himself in to authorities in 1999. His given name was Angel Maturino Resendez.

Among the victims were Jesse Howell and Wendy Von Huben, two teenage runaways. Resendez-Ramirez bludgeoned Howell to death and left the body next to the railroad tracks near Belleview, Florida. Von Huben's remains were found after Resendez-Ramirez's arrest. He admitted to raping her, strangling her, and sodomizing her body, according to *Oxygen*.

He later bludgeoned Christopher Maier to death. Maier was a student at the University of Kentucky. He then raped and beat Maier's girlfriend, Holly Dunn. Dunn survived the attack.

In 1998, Resendez-Ramirez murdered three more people across Georgia and Texas. He broke into people's homes, mostly near train tracks. In Georgia, he killed Leafie Mason, 87, with an antique flat iron, according to *Oxygen*. He bludgeoned Fannie Whitney Byers, 81. Back in Texas, he raped and murdered Claudia Benton, who worked as a pediatric neurologist.

He was known as the Railroad Killer because authorities thought he traveled town-to-town hopping freight trains to find his victims. He also used trains to find farm work in the Midwest and the South, according to *Oxygen*.[83]

Resendez-Ramirez had a long criminal history before he

was arrested for murder. He'd been in trouble for burglary, aggravated assault, and felony possession of a firearm in several states. He'd been deported a handful of times and spent time locked up in US prisons. He was a drifter.

He was raised by his single mother until he was six, according to *Oxygen*. Then he was sent to live with his aunt and uncle for a time. When he was around 12 years old, he returned to live with his mother.

The village where his aunt lived didn't have a high school, so returning to his mother seemed to be the best option. But Resendez-Ramirez didn't seem to make it to high school. He finished out the seventh grade, and that seems to be the end of his education.

When he was about 13 or 14, he was sexually assaulted by a group of older boys, his mother told the *Chicago Tribune*. His mother said he was also gang-raped in prison in the US.[84]

Resendez-Ramirez did have some normalcy in his life. He had a common-law wife and a baby girl at the time of the murders, according to the *Chicago Tribune*. Even with a baby coming into the world, Resendez-Ramirez kept killing. He broke into another Texas home in spring of 1999. He killed Norman Sirnic and his wife, Karen, with a sledgehammer.

On June 4, 1999, Resendez-Ramirez broke into Noemi Dominguez's apartment in Houston. He raped her before bludgeoning her to death with a pickaxe. She'd been a school-teacher. He stole her car and used the same pickaxe to kill

Josephine Konvicka in Fayette County, Texas.

After a six-week manhunt that made him a well-known fugitive, he turned himself in. He'd been hiding out in Mexico but surrendered to a Texas Ranger at an El Paso border station. The deal was brokered by his sister, according to *Intelligencer Journal* archives.[85]

Rookie Texas Ranger Sgt. Drew Carter had established some rapport with Resendez-Ramirez's sister a couple weeks prior to the arrest when Carter and another Ranger had interviewed her, according to the *Chicago Tribune*.

She called Sgt. Carter, who had been on vacation, to tell him she'd been talking to her brother through an intermediary. Sgt. Carter, an FBI agent, and a US Marshal Service inspector headed to New Mexico to hash out a deal. Key demands included promises of Resendez-Ramirez's personal safety while in jail, regular visiting rights, and a psychological evaluation, according to the *Tribune*. The deal didn't include protection from the death penalty.

She then persuaded her brother to walk from Ciudad Juarez in Mexico to surrender. Sgt. Carter met him on the bridge with a handshake and then handcuffs, according to *Monitor* archives.[86]

"The family always urged him to turn himself in because he was ruining our lives," said his aunt, Augustina Solis de Resendiz in an interview with the *Tribune*. But she added, "I feel bad because whatever has happened, he is still family."

Law enforcement ended up awarding his sister $86,000 for helping in his capture.

Police found fingerprints on a woman's stolen car that matched Resendez-Ramirez, and DNA evidence also linked him to the murders.

On June 27, 2006, Resendez-Ramirez was executed by lethal injection. According to NBC News, his last words included a prayer.[87]

"I want to ask if it is in your heart to forgive me," he said, looking at the relatives of the victims who were in another room. "You don't have to. I know I allowed the devil to rule my life."

"I deserve what I am getting," he said just before he died.

Rory Conde

Rory Conde, a Colombian native, killed at least six women in Miami, Florida, in 1994.

He earned himself the moniker "Tamiami Strangler" after preying on prostitutes along Miami's Tamiami Trail. He'd pick them up along a stretch of rundown motels, murder them, then dump their bodies in suburban neighborhoods.

At least once, he taunted police—much like how Joe made calls before his attacks—by leaving a "catch-me-if-you-can" message on one victim's back, according to a report by the Associated Press.

Conde was also a shoplifter. In a roundabout way, that

was his downfall.

He left a woman he'd bound with duct tape in his apartment while he went to court to deal with a shoplifting charge. The woman was able to get the neighbor's attention.

One of his victims included a transgender woman. In court, Conde's defense argued that he snapped when he learned that the prostitute he was having sex with was transgender. It brought back memories of childhood sexual abuse Conde suffered, his defense argued.

Before the murders, Conde was married and had two children. When his wife discovered he had been sleeping with prostitutes, she left him.

Aileen Wuornos

There have been many female serial killers throughout history, as well as male. Aileen Wuornos is one of them. Wuornos killed at least seven men between 1989 and 1990. She shot her victims point-blank in the face. She worked as a prostitute and claimed, at least at first, that she had killed those men to protect herself.

Her first victim was a man named Richard Mallory, a convicted rapist. He worked as a television repair shop owner, according to the *Asbury Park Press* archives. According to Wuornos, he was abusive, and they got into a scuffle.[88]

According to court documents, police found Mallory's body miles away from his abandoned vehicle in a wooded area.

He'd been shot several times, but two bullets to the left lung were found to ultimately cause his death. The medical examiner found he'd been drinking before his death.

She shot a concrete company worker, a Tennessee rodeo worker, and a missionary. "He was gonna rape me, maybe even kill me," Wuornos said of the missionary, according to the *Press*. "...Nobody would have believed he hurt me, so I killed him." She later killed a sausage company delivery man, a retired police chief, and a former security guard and truck driver.

According to the *Press* article, she had a method. She always used condoms. She got undressed first. She tried not to go too far back into the woods. She wanted to be able to see the road. She made sure to unzip her purse, so she could grab her .22 handgun if she needed to.

"If I had wanted to kill just anybody, I had lots of chances," she said, according to the *Press*.

She was diagnosed by defense psychiatrists with borderline personality disorder and antisocial personality disorder, but she was still sentenced to death. She died by lethal injection in October 2002.

Wuornos had been raised by her grandparents. Her father was in prison for committing sex crimes against a child. He had raped a seven-year-old girl, according to the *Asbury Park Press* archives. Her mother had skipped town when Aileen was just six months old, leaving Wuornos and her brother behind.

In court, Wuornos said her grandfather beat her and

raped her, and eventually her brother did too. By the time she turned 11, she was trading sex for cigarettes and more with her classmates.

When she was around 13, one of her grandfather's friends raped her and got her pregnant. No one believed she'd been raped. She was sent to a home for unwed mothers by her grandparents, who decided she was wild and boy crazy, according to the *Press*. Once she had the baby, she put him up for adoption.

She came back home for a short while, but her grandmother died of liver failure, and it all fell apart. Her grandfather kicked her out of her home. She turned to prostitution to make a living.

In court, Wuornos' uncle, Barry, disputed her claims that she'd been abused by her grandfather, according to *Florida Today* archives. "We were a pretty straight and normal family—very little trouble in the family," Barry told the jury in 1992.

Barry said his father was a "gentle man. He laid down strong rules, but [he was] a man you could look up to." He also denied his father had a drinking problem.[89]

Barry told the court Wuornos started getting into trouble when she was around 10 or 11, about the time he left home to join the military. She got in trouble for things such as shoplifting and setting a small fire that burned her around the face, according to *Florida Today*.

When she turned 20, Wuornos married a 70-year-old man who had picked her up hitchhiking. The marriage ended after about a month, with both parties claiming they had been beaten by the other.

When she was 22, according to the *Press*, Wuornos shot herself in the stomach as part of her sixth suicide attempt in 10 years. She told a psychiatrist then she'd been raped and beaten a dozen times.

Wuornos started dating a woman named Tyria Moore around 1987. Moore worked as a maid. One day when she was drunk, Wuornos told Moore she'd shot and killed a man that morning, according to court documents. She told Moore she sorted through the man's things, kept some, and threw the rest out. According to the *Press*, Wuornos then acted as if it were a joke. It's possible that, for a time, Moore believed it was one.

In the end, it was a careless joyride that did Wuornos in. Someone saw Wuornos and Moore driving one of the dead men's cars, a Pontiac Sunbird. The two had taken it for a drive and then crashed the car into someone's front gate, according to the *Press*.

People rushed to help them, worried they were hurt, but then Wuornos denied having anything to do with the car. She and Moore walked off down the highway. That made people suspicious. She'd also left behind a bloody handprint.

Months later, Moore saw media reports saying that police

were looking for two women suspected of being involved in several murders, according to court documents. In a panic, Moore left Wuornos and took off to her old home in Pennsylvania. Police tracked down Moore and convinced her to work with them, telling her she'd be cleared of wrongdoing if she got Wuornos to confess. Moore was successful.

"Sure, I shot them, but it was self-defense," Wuornos said in a jailhouse confession, according to the *Asbury Park Press*. "I've been raped 12 times in the last eight years and I just got sick of it. So, I got this gun and was carrying it around. As soon as I got the gun, it got worse."

Wuornos took money and valuables from the dead men and threw things like their IDs in the woods. Police found a rented storage bin where she kept the items she had taken from the men she killed, such as Super Bowl playing cards, alarm clocks, and a fishing reel, according to the *Press*. Police also found a briefcase with her .22 revolver, handcuffs, and a flashlight. She'd dumped it in Rose Bay near the South Daytona strip.

Wuornos was sentenced to death and was killed by lethal injection in October 2002. Her last words were, "I'll be back."

CHAPTER 18

EVADING CAPTURE

Many of these crimes took place around the same time period. The 1970s, 1980s, and 1990s saw a rise in murder rates across the country—committed by serial killers or otherwise.

According to a report put out by the US Department of Justice in 2011, the homicide rate doubled from the early 1960s to the late 1970s, increasing from 4.6 per 100,000 US residents in 1962 to 9.7 per 100,000 by 1979. In 1980, the rate peaked at 10.2 per 100,000 people. It fell to 7.9 per 100,000 people in 1984, before rising again in the late 1980s and early 1990s.

According to the Radford database, 1989 was the year the number of serial killers peaked with 193 separate serial killers operating in the US.[90] The homicide rate saw another peak of 9.8 per 100,000 people in 1991. Homicides saw a sharp decline after that. By 2010, the homicide rate had fallen to 4.8 per 100,000 people, per the report.

According to the Radford database, an average of 43 serial

killers have been identified in the US each year in the last decade. No one knows for sure why there is such a sharp rise in crime or why serial killers are so prevalent at certain times.

Four decades ago, about one-third of serial killers could get away with five or more murders before they got caught, according to an analysis by *Vox*.[91] Today, only about 13% of serial killers can get away with five or more victims. More than half are caught after two killings. Experts have several theories about why.

POLICE SYSTEMS

Police were not as organized in those decades. It took time for different departments to interact and connect the dots. That's true for Joe's case.

Investigators acknowledge that poor communication between agencies contributed to the difficulty they had catching Joe. Many different departments worked in silos, investigating the Cordova Cat Burglar, the Visalia Ransacker, the East Area Rapist, and the Original Night Stalker; for decades, law enforcement believed these crimes were committed by different people.

Rivalries were alive and real between departments, and another factor was a very real lack of trust between departments. It was long suspected that the attacker was a police officer. No one wanted to accidentally tip off the bad guy, so they clammed up.

"We couldn't be sure about the guy volunteering from the neighboring agencies," Wendell Phillips, a former Sacramento County sheriff's deputy told the *Los Angeles Times* in 2018. "There was concern about sharing information because, let's face it, loose lips sink ships."[92]

Things were so disconnected that news of Joe being fired from the Auburn Police Department for shoplifting never made it to the East Area Rapist task force, according to the *Times*, despite the fact that they were on the look-out for an ex-cop.

During Joe's alleged crimes, police didn't use DNA technology yet. The internet was just getting its legs. Big criminal databases didn't exist yet either. But that's all different now.

In an interview with the *Guardian*, Aamodt said he thinks one of the biggest reasons for the decline is changes in the parole system.

"Not quite 20% of our serial killers were people who had killed, gone to prison and had been released and killed again. With the longer prison sentences and the reduction in parole, those folks are not going to be back on the streets to kill again," he told the *Guardian*.[93]

BEHAVIOR CHANGE

Aamodt told the *Guardian* that people have changed their behavior significantly from the 1970s too.

"[We] would hitchhike, we would let kids walk to the store, let 'em go play," he said. "If there was a stranded motorist you'd go and help them—we don't do those things anymore."

Granted, people don't need to hitchhike like they used to. Cars were harder to come by back in the 1970s. People trusted strangers more.

By the 1980s, horror movies hyped up the fear of the psychopathic hitchhiker. It signaled the beginning of the end of an era.

Parents don't let their kids wander around unsupervised as much these days. We're more likely to take an Uber than to hitchhike. We now believe that horrible crimes can and do happen to people like us.

HIGHWAYS

Some speculate the creation of interstate highways played a role in the spike of serial killer activity. It became relatively easy for murderers to travel from state to state, leaving behind bodies. This was a time before social media and 24-hour news networks, and it was relatively easy for someone like Ted Bundy to drift into a new town where no one suspected a thing.

The FBI set up a system called the Highway Serial Killings Initiative, which it announced publicly in 2009. It started in 2004 when an FBI analyst noticed a pattern—bodies of women turning up along the Interstate 40 corridor in Oklahoma,

Texas, Arkansas, and Mississippi.

Most of the victims were women living "high-risk, transient lifestyles," according to the FBI. The victims were often picked up at truck stops or service stations only to be sexually assaulted, murdered, and dumped along the highway.

The agency also established the National Center for the Analysis of Violent Crime. The database now tracks homicides, sexual assaults, missing persons, and unidentified human remains across the country, allowing law enforcement a better chance to connect the dots when crimes cross jurisdictions. A report by the *Los Angeles Times* explains how the database helps the FBI track suspicious deaths and suspect truckers.[94]

It helped law enforcement link several cases to a man named John Robert Williams in 2008. Williams and his girlfriend kidnapped a woman from a casino in Mississippi, according to the *Times*, before killing her and dumping her body along a rural stretch of road. Williams' girlfriend panicked and called police. She told them they found the body, but law enforcement quickly found holes in her story.

It turns out, Williams would later confess to more than 30 murders. He was sentenced to life in prison in 2007. His girlfriend, Rachel Cumberland, was sentenced to 20 years in prison. She served eight of her 20 years before being released.

The initiative has also helped the FBI spot patterns in real time and catch killers, as with the case of Bruce Mendenhall. According to a story in the *Chicago Tribune*, Mendenhall was a Vietnam vet who was married and had at least two children.

He even ran for mayor of Albion, Illinois in 1997.

Several prostitutes were found dead along the highway across Georgia and Tennessee around 2007. They'd been shot with a .22-caliber gun. Thanks to the database, one Nashville homicide detective knew there was a pattern to the murders. He looked through hours of video footage of trucks pulling in and out of the truck stop where one victim was found until he spotted something odd.

The *Los Angeles Times* reported that the detective noticed that one truck pulled in and out more quickly than the others. On a hunch, the detective approached the truck in a nearby town after watching the tape. When Mendenhall opened the door, he looked disheveled. The detective noticed some drops of blood on Mendenhall thumb and on the door. Upon further inspection, the detective found women's clothing and an ATM card that belonged to a woman who'd gone missing 12 hours earlier. Mendenhall later told authorities he'd murdered six women near truck stops in Tennessee, Indiana, Georgia, and Alabama, according to the *Chicago Tribune*.[95]

According to the FBI, since the initiative launched, it's helped solve many cases that might otherwise have been difficult for local law enforcement to piece together.

LEAD EXPOSURE

Some experts suggest lead exposure, especially by petrol, could have impacted the crime rate in this era. The human body can't really tell the difference between lead and calcium. The body needs calcium to work properly, especially in the central nervous system. When lead gets in the system, it messes with brain development and neurotransmitter functions, meaning that it impacts cognition, attention, and memory.

According to the Brookings Institute, the idea is that "lead exposure at young ages leaves children with learning disabilities, ADHD, and impulse control problems; and those problems cause them to commit crime as adults—particularly violent crime."

In one study, researchers Anna Aizer and Janet Currie analyzed the lead levels in the blood of 120,000 children born between 1990 and 2004 in Rhode Island.

They found a strong link between childhood lead exposure and antisocial behavior, which was later associated with more school suspensions, juvenile detention rates, and higher incarceration rates later in life. For years, many kids got exposed to lead through paint, leaded gasoline, and sometimes water.

Epidemiologists took notice of this in the 1970s, realizing that high lead levels cause all kinds of problems. The EPA started to crack down on various companies between 1975 and 1985 for exposing kids to lead. Eventually, lead was removed from gasoline in most places in the world, resulting in less exposure.

According to a National Bureau of Economic Research summary of Aizer and Currie's findings, the two concluded

"...[their] results support the hypothesis that reductions in blood lead levels may indeed have been responsible for a significant part of the observed decrease in antisocial behavior among youths and young adults in recent decades."

Others are skeptical of giving lead so much credit for the rise and subsequent fall of crime rates. Wayne Hall, a researcher at The University of Queensland Centre for Clinical Research in Australia analyzed data from several different studies in a 2013 article published in the US National Library of Medicine. He came to a different conclusion.

"Lead exposure in childhood may have played a small role in rising and falling crime rates in the USA but it is unlikely to account for the very high percentage of the decline," Hall wrote.

MASS SHOOTINGS

Some crime experts believe that modern mass shootings have replaced the serial killers of the 1970s and 1980s.

Stephen Paddock opened fire on concertgoers in Las Vegas on October 1, 2017. He killed 58 people and injured about 700. The act itself took between 10 and 15 minutes.

Omar Saddiqui Mateen killed 49 people and injured 50 in the Pulse nightclub in Orlando, Florida, June 12, 2016.

Seung-Hui Cho killed 32 people at the Virginia Tech campus on April 16, 2007.

Adam Lanza killed 20 children and six adults at Sandy

Hook Elementary School December 14, 2012.

Those are just a handful of the deadliest mass shootings.

Scott Bonn, a criminologist and author of *Why We Love Serial Killers: The Curious Appeal of the World's Most Savage Murderers*, spoke with the *Mercury News* about the shift.[96]

"Mass shooters are the new serial killers in many ways," Bonn said. "What did the '70s become known as? The 'me' decade. You had these serial killers who said, 'You will know me.' These narcissistic, self-aggrandizing serial killers emerged out of that environment.

"Today, you have a very different kind of predator out there," Bonn said. "Since 9/11, there's been an environment of fear. We live in a very divisive political environment now, where many groups feel disenfranchised. This alienation that I believe exists today has percolated and exploded to a point where individuals who have certain grievances are taking it out on the streets and on society in general."

Serial killers are still around, of course, Bonn told the *Mercury News*, but the trend has dissipated in the last 25 years, "…whereas a pattern of mass public shooters has increased in the last 25 years," Bonn said. "They're still relatively rare, but we're seeing on average one every four weeks."

IMPACT OF WAR

Peter Vronsky, an investigative historian, author, and filmmaker based in Canada, argues in his book, *Sons of Cain: A History of Serial Killers from the Stone Age to the Present*, that World War II could have been a factor.

Vronsky examined serial killers and their childhoods for more than 30 years. Many serial killers, he noticed, were children during World War II. Many of their fathers fought in the war. Many suffered abuse at the hands of their fathers, who returned from war traumatized. According to Vronsky, there was a spike in serial killings between 1935 and 1950, after World War I, though it was less pronounced.

Canadian criminologist Michael Arntfield spoke to the BBC about the spike of serial killer activities in the 1970s and 1980s. Arntfield said he sees similar trends emerging in society now—social upheaval, the 2008 financial crisis, wars, and terrorism. He speculates the combined social forces might usher in another spike in serial killings in the next few decades.

"We are living in the throes of an equally tumultuous and polarizing time," Arntfield told the BBC, "and that immediately gave way to the 'golden age' of the serial killer."

WHY ARE WE SO INTERESTED?

Americans are fascinated with serial killers. True crime books, podcasts, movies, shows, and more abound. People always want to know more—more gory details, more clues, more reasons, more explanations.

In 2019, 30 years after his death, several movies came out

about Ted Bundy. *Conversations with a Killer: The Ted Bundy Tapes* is a Netflix documentary that features interviews with Bundy while he sat on death row.

Extremely Wicked, Shockingly Evil and Vile is another Bundy flick that came out in 2019. It features Zac Efron and Lily Collins, telling the story of Bundy's crimes from the perspective of Liz, his long-time girlfriend.

In 2003, the movie *Monster* featured Aileen Wuornos's story. There were several pieces made dramatizing her life even before she was put to death.

My Friend Dahmer came out in 2017, depicting Jeffery Dahmer as a shy kid who later becomes a murderer.

There's even a Crime Museum open in Washington, DC. It was established in 2008 to serve as an "educational resource on law enforcement, crime history, and forensic science," according to its website. Some of John Wayne Gacy's clown suits are on display, alongside Ted Bundy's Volkswagen Bug.[97]

I imagine that it won't be long before a movie is made about Joe's life.

I know I'm just scratching the surface of movies based on real serial killers. There are probably hundreds, if not thousands, out there. That doesn't even include movies like *The Silence of the Lambs*, which came out in 1991.

According to the FBI, we're 12 times more likely to be killed by a family member than a serial killer. Less than 1% of murders in this country are committed by serial killers.

Domestic violence, which is far more common and often deadly, just doesn't captivate the public like serial murder.

I think we're so interested because deep down, we all want to know why. Why did this happen? How was it possible for someone to commit a crime like this? What makes them different? How are we the same?

I think, in part, we want to believe people who can commit such atrocities are nothing like us. We want to believe we'd see them coming. We want to believe we aren't in danger. We want to believe we can figure out why it happened so it doesn't happen again.

"We demand answers," Scott Bonn writes. "What we get back from the media and law enforcement is: 'Evil has come to our town, but don't worry about it, we're going to conquer evil.' That narrative in some ways is reassuring, but it's reassuring in a way that's not real. It's an oversimplification, but it's done so that we feel better."

CHAPTER 19

THE AFTERMATH

In the weeks after Joe was arrested, I noticed police cars around me everywhere I went.

One day, I drove from the RV park in Orangevale where I was staying to Folsom to get a haircut. It was on the way, as I planned to visit one of my daughters later that day. I waited for about 10 minutes before the hairdresser seated me. We had a lively conversation. I told her about my travels and learned a bit about what was going on in her life—typical haircut chatter.

Then the phone rang. Another hairdresser answered and after a short conversation, my hairdresser was called to the phone. She left for a moment to take the call. When she returned, she was jarringly quiet. She stopped chatting with me and just finished cutting my hair. She seemed spooked, but I didn't know why. I didn't want to pry into her personal life, so I just let it be and tried to mind my own business. We didn't talk much after her call.

She seemed happier as I paid her and headed out.

Over the next couple days, I saw no police cars around. I never got any proof, but I wondered if they took some of that hair to use for DNA samples. Police and the public speculated then that Joe had an accomplice. Maybe they were suspicious of me.

About a week later, a detective called me to talk about Joe. I answered whatever questions he asked to the best of my ability.

I told the detective what I thought about police trying to collect my DNA. He didn't confirm anything, but he did chuckle.

I even went back to the hair salon a few weeks later to see if my hairdresser had been on the phone with police. I was too late, though; she'd been transferred somewhere else.

Though I never got the incident confirmed, I don't believe in coincidences. I know I saw police officers on just about every street corner before that day, and after, they all seemed to disappear. I would have given over my DNA voluntarily, but law enforcement never asked for it.

The detective mostly asked me about what I knew about Joe's work history after he was fired from the Auburn Police Department. I learned that Joe lied on his last application. He said he'd worked for Terra Nova Produce—a company I worked for—but he never had. Terra Nova Produce went broke, so no one from the company would have been able to dispute the claim he worked there.

I told the detective that Joe talked about truck repair school and claimed that he had gotten a settlement for retraining, but that I doubted the settlement part was true. I also told him I doubted that Joe had an accomplice. I don't think he would have risked anyone keeping his secret safe, because his life depended on those secrets.

There are plenty of armchair detectives out there who still think Joe had an accomplice throughout his crime spree. Reddit threads abound with internet sleuths determined to make Sharon or Joe's brother, John, out to be part of the whole thing. Detectives say that whether Joe had an accomplice remains an open question.

Some victims reported that they heard their attacker speaking to another person. According to the *Sacramento Bee*, victims heard him say things like, "Take this to the car" or "I thought I told you to shut up." But he may have been saying those things to confuse people. He often lied to victims and made things up to confuse people.[98]

Paul Holes told the *Bee* he thought it was possible Joe had an accomplice during some of his earlier crimes. But "...when he ends up escalating into homicide, I think that's just him," Holes told the *Bee*.

The Sacramento County Sheriff's Department, on the other hand, came out saying that Joe is the sole suspect behind all the crimes.

Holes told the *Bee* that even if Joe did have an accomplice, that accomplice would probably be dead. "If there was a second person, I think [the East Area Rapist] would have just killed him [to tie up loose ends]," Holes said.

It's been more than a year since the arrest. At first, I was flooded with calls from unknown numbers. Reporters were constantly asking for interviews.

I had my phone number up on Facebook for a while, so I was easy to reach. At the time, I figured I didn't have anything to hide, so I didn't want to shrink back. I gave a handful of interviews in the beginning, but I still didn't really know what to say.

I even got offered a trip to New York to be interviewed on the *Today* show, but I declined that interview. Knowing how my senior mind works these days, I was worried I'd misspeak or forget some important details.

Reporters slowly stopped calling. To be fair, I don't answer if I don't know the number either.

But I realize the public-at-large wants answers about this horrific criminal's life.

After the arrest, I spent time researching the Golden State Killer's crimes because I never had before. They'd always seemed like something happening in the background, involving faraway people I didn't know. I was scared of the East Area Rapist for a while, but that was nothing compared to the terror his victims felt.

After a few months of researching and writing down anything I could remember about Joe, I decided I had little doubt at all that Joe was the man behind the crimes. I decided he didn't deserve to be put away quietly.

I want him to start paying for what he's done. He murdered and hurt so many people who never did anything to him. He had no reason to commit a single crime. That pisses me off and breaks my heart at the same time.

I'd say he had a very good and fulfilling life, so I'm all the more disturbed.

He had a family who loved him. He had friends who cared about him. He could have been a decent person. Yet he decided to commit some of the most heinous crimes imaginable.

No one in our family suspected a thing. When we found out, we were all devastated.

My mom has been visibly upset and hurt by the revelation. Joe was like another son to her. He often came over to help her out with small projects around the house. Even after he and Sharon split, my mom always welcomed him.

Nicole, who spent so much of her childhood at Joe's house, still finds it hard to think of him as anything other than Uncle Joe—she still has trouble accepting it.

For Deanna, many of her childhood memories are forever tainted by the truth that's come to light.

Some of my family encouraged me to write this book. They knew this whole thing would continue to eat away at me if I didn't. Some of my family wishes I hadn't.

I know it will take years and years for others in my family to be ready to talk about Joe. They're struggling to come to terms with what happened and want to stay silent at this time. Maybe they'll speak out years from now.

I won't hold their silence against them. Someday, when they're ready to talk, I'm sure the world will still be listening.

As for me, this book has been my way to make sense of it all.

While I stayed in town for a couple months after the news first broke, I'm back on the road. RV life suits me. I love being able to travel.

I have traveled from Washington State to Acadia National Park in Maine. I love how the view is constantly changing. I like to set up camp for the night or a week, mostly in dispersed federal or state properties. I get to meet all kinds of different people from across the country and even some folks from Canada. During my travels, I met a Canadian from Thunder Bay who happened to share my birthday. For the last three years, Ken and I have visited and enjoyed a birthday dinner together. Most of the time, I see fellow campers once or maybe twice and then they head off chasing their own adventure. But it's nice to see a familiar face every now and then.

I've spent some time in Mexico, too. It's easy to get down there while I'm already spending time in Yuma, Arizona. I learned I can save a chunk of change on dental work over there.

I plan to spend this fall exploring New Mexico. I want to head to Carlsbad Caverns. Maybe I'll head to White Sands National Monument or check out the Albuquerque International Balloon Fiesta. Then maybe I'll head up to British Columbia or explore around Alaska.

I love travel photography. When I go to new places, I'll try to take one or two good photos. I like to send them to my girls and keep in touch no matter where I end up.

I put off a couple big trips so I could write this book and get it out into the world. Since I began the writing process, I have driven fewer than 6,000 miles. In years prior, I was clocking in 12,000 to 15,000 miles in the RV. I'm anxious to get back on the road and back to my life as I finish this book.

Since I started piecing together as much as I can remember, I've been sleeping better. I don't wake up in the middle of the night thinking of all the things Joe and I used to do together. But I still wonder how I could have missed it. I think back to the signs and clues that have added meaning now: how neat and tidy he was, his arrogance, the road rage incident and his explosive anger, the gold bars, his issues with affection and declaration that Bonnie was the love of his life, his boast that he knows "how to get rid of someone." I only saw the good side. I only saw the man I considered a brother for more than 40 years.

I still don't have the answers. I don't know if there are two Joes or if he knew what he was doing the whole time. Either way, I think he genuinely loved his daughters and cared for my mom. I want to think, at least for a time, that he valued my friendship.

But he betrayed me. He betrayed Sharon. He betrayed my parents, my children, and his children. That's something I must grapple with.

I have wondered why he didn't come after me. He had no issue attacking men and women alike. I think he thought that he was invincible then, having been a police officer and gone to college. I think it's most likely because police would have suspected someone in the family. It would have been inconvenient for him.

I tend to believe he was so confident he could get away with murder and all his other crimes with calculated, deliberate disregard that his only concern was getting caught. That was a good reason to stop being a criminal after he learned about the possibilities that DNA evidence afforded to law enforcement.

I think he was playing a game and he thought he could outsmart everyone—the police, his coworkers, his wife, his children, and his friends. He got lucky in all the worst ways for a long time. But his luck ran out.

I might never know for sure, but I hope in some way this book helps to punch back. I hope to expose who he was as a person, as best as I can remember. I want to expose any parts of him that might help victims heal, or help people understand him better. Maybe this will even help other folks recognize a hidden predator in their own lives, though I know better than most how well a hunter can hide in plain sight.

If any of the details I've shared make him mad, I'll be glad for it. I hope it'll shake him up enough to spill the rest of his secrets.

The trial is set to take place in Sacramento. It's expected to cost taxpayers $20 million and could take up to 10 years.

Joe's in his 70s now. He will likely live to be convicted or die an innocent man. I think prosecutors should consider that, as the court date remains undecided at the time this book was written.

Prosecutors from the six different counties where the Golden State Killer is believed to have committed his crimes—Contra Costa, Tulare, Santa Barbara, Ventura, Orange, and Sacramento—agreed to work together on a joint trial through the Sacramento County District Attorney's Office. It's expected to be the biggest case in California history.

Joe will be represented by a public defender.

Though I considered him a friend for more than 40 years, I hope he pays for what he did. I hope his victims will know peace.

ENDNOTES

CHAPTER 1

1 Jason Silverstein, "Joseph James DeAngelo, Golden Gate Killer Suspect, Once Asked Relative About Serial Rapes," *Oxygen*, April 25, 2018, https://www.oxygen.com/joseph-james-deangelo-golden-state-killer-relative-rapes.

CHAPTER 2

2 Newspapers.com, "Joseph James DeAngelo Sr, air force duty 1951," accessed November 15, 2019, https://www.newspapers.com/clip/19573789/joseph_james_deangelo_sr_air_force/.

3 Newspapers.com, "Star-Gazette from Elmira, New York, May 25, 1944," accessed January 22, 2020, https://www.newspapers.com/newspage/276390304/.

4 Paige St. John, "Man in the Window," *Los Angeles Times*, accessed November 15, 2019, https://www.latimes.com/projects/man-in-the-window-joe-DeAngelo-golden-state-killer-serial/.

CHAPTER 3

5 Cold Case Investigations Unit, "East Area Rapist/Maggiore Murder Case," Arcgis.com, accessed November 15, 2019, https://www.arcgis.com/apps/MapJournal/index.html?appid=4212543183b848e88d3432f5147321f6.

6 Paige St. John, "Man in the Window," LATimes.com.

7 Benjamin Oreskes and Richard Winton, "Golden State Killer Suspect May Be Linked to Earlier Cordova Cat Burglar Attacks," *Los Angeles Times*, May 11, 2018, https://www.latimes.com/local/lanow/la-me-ln-cat-golden-state-killer-20180510-story.html.

CHAPTER 4

8   Oreskes and Winton, "Golden State Killer Suspect."

9   Cold Case Investigations Unit, "East Area Rapist/Maggiore Murder Case."

10   Cold Case Investigations Unit, "East Area Rapist/Maggiore Murder Case."

CHAPTER 5

11   Cold Case Investigations Unit, "East Area Rapist/Maggiore Murder Case."

12   Joseph Serna, Richard Winton, Sarah Parvini, "As a Young Cop, Golden State Killer Suspect Was Aloof, Ambitious, 'Always Serious,'" *Los Angeles Times*, May 1, 2018, https://www.latimes.com/local/lanow/la-me-golden-state-cops-20180501-story.html.

13   Serna, Winton, and Parvini, "As a Young Cop."

14   "Golden State Killer Suspect Joseph James DeAngelo Redacted Arrest Warrant," contributed by Chris Hagan, Capital Public Radio, DocumentCloud, accessed January 24, 2020, https://www.documentcloud.org/documents/4492711-P-v-DeAngelo-Redacted-Arrest-Warrant-Final.html, 9.

15   Sam Stanton, Darryl Smith and Lewis Griswold, "Tulare County officials charge East Area Rapist suspect in 1975 Visalia slaying," *Sacramento Bee,* August 13, 2018, accessed March 5, 2020, https://www.sacbee.com/news/local/crime/article216586495.html

CHAPTER 6

16   Redacted arrest warrant, Joseph James DeAngelo, 9.

17   FBI, "First Survivor of East Area Rapist/Serial Killer Recalls Encounter," KTVU, April 25, 2018, accessed January 29, 2020 https://www.youtube.com/watch?v=XKFLM627KWY

18   Redacted arrest warrant, Joseph James DeAngelo, 11.

19   Redacted arrest warrant, Joseph James DeAngelo, 12.

20   Redacted arrest warrant, Joseph James DeAngelo, 13–14.

21   Redacted arrest warrant, Joseph James DeAngelo, 15.

22   Redacted arrest warrant, Joseph James DeAngelo, 15–16.

CHAPTER 7

23   Redacted arrest warrant, Joseph James DeAngelo, 30.

24   Redacted arrest warrant, Joseph James DeAngelo, 17–18.

25   Redacted arrest warrant, Joseph James DeAngelo, 18–20.

26   Redacted arrest warrant, Joseph James DeAngelo, 20–22.

27   Redacted arrest warrant, Joseph James DeAngelo, 22–23.

28   Redacted arrest warrant, Joseph James DeAngelo, 23–26.

29   Redacted arrest warrant, Joseph James DeAngelo, 12–13.

30   Newspapers.com, "Rapist Hits 17th Victim," *Sacramento Bee,* March 20, 1977, https://www.newspapers.com/image/620900254/

CHAPTER 8

31   United Press International, "Sacramento Rapist Hits in Stockton" *Napa Valley Register,* March 7, 1977 https://www.newspapers.com/image/563937574/?terms=East%2BArea%2BRapist

32   Redacted arrest warrant, Joseph James DeAngelo, 13.

33   Redacted arrest warrant, Joseph James DeAngelo, 27–28.

34   Redacted arrest warrant, Joseph James DeAngelo, 30–33.

35   Redacted arrest warrant, Joseph James DeAngelo, 34.

36   Newspapers.com, "East Area Rapist Strikes Second Time in Stockton," *Los Angeles Times,* March 20, 1978, https://www.newspapers.com/image/384321183/?terms=East%2BArea%2BRapist.

37   Newspapers.com, "Sacramento Rapist Strikes," *Times-Advocate*, April 16, 1978, https://www.newspapers.com/image/569180349/?terms=East%2BArea%2BRapist.

38   Newspapers.com, "Sacramento Rapist Claims 33rd Victim," *San Francisco Examiner*, April 16, 1978, https://www.newspapers.com/image/460525758/?terms=East%2BArea%2BRapist.

CHAPTER 9

39 Redacted arrest warrant, Joseph James DeAngelo, 38.

40 Redacted arrest warrant, Joseph James DeAngelo, 39–41.

41 Don Lattin, "The Most Terrifying Thing about East Area Rapist Is Not the Act," *San Francisco Examiner*, June 26, 1979, https://www.newspapers.com/image/461119567/?terms=East%2BArea%2BRapist%2Bluncheon.

42 Newspapers.com, "August 29," *Auburn Journal*, December 31, 1979, https://www.newspapers.com/image/378735843/?terms=Joseph%2BJames%2BDeAngelo%2Btrial.

43 Newspapers.com, "Capital Court Ponders Auburn Policeman Fate," *Auburn Journal*, October 26, 1979, https://www.newspapers.com/image/378721340/?terms=Joseph%2BDeAngelo.

44 Newspapers.com, "Jury Finds Policeman Guilty of Shoplifting," *Auburn Journal*, October 31, 1979, https://www.newspapers.com/image/378722574/?terms=Joseph%2BDeAngelo.

45 Newspapers.com, "News in Brief," *Los Angeles Times, April 6, 1979,* https://www.newspapers.com/image/387596767/?terms=East%2BArea%2BRapist

46 Newspapers.com, "Neighbors Arming after Rapist Attack," *San Francisco Examiner*, June 12, 1979, https://www.newspapers.com/image/461137844/?terms=East%2BArea%2BRapist.

47 Lattin, "The Most Terrifying Thing."

48 Newspapers.com, "Murders Blamed on Burglar," *Santa Maria Times,* January 30, 1980, https://www.newspapers.com/image/446921866

49 Newspapers.com, "1979 County Homicides Totaled 27," Santa Maria Times, January 30, 1980, https://www.newspapers.com/image/446966774/?terms=Robert%2BOfferman.

50 Newspapers.com, "Slain Attorney, Wife Were Beaten to Death," *San Bernardino County Sun*, March 19, 1980, https://www.newspapers.com/image/63199443/?terms=Lyman%2BSmith.

51 Redacted arrest warrant, Joseph James DeAngelo, 43–45.

52 Gary Jarlson, "Families of Slain Couple Offer $25,000 to Find Killer," *Los Angeles Times*, September 19, 1980, https://www.newspapers.com/image/387137207/?terms=Keith%2BHarrington.

CHAPTER 10

53   Redacted arrest warrant, Joseph James DeAngelo, 44.

54   Brad Hunter, "Golden State Killer Tormented Victim's Hubby for Decades,"
     Toronto Sun, May 8, 2018, https://torontosun.com/news/world/golden-state-
     killer-tormented-victims-hubby-for-decades.

55   Newspapers.com, "Goleta Double Murder Discovered," *Santa
     Maria Times*, July 28, 1981, https://www.newspapers.com/
     image/446910182/?terms=Cheri%2BDomingo.

56   Eric Malnic, "Tie Hinted in Pair of Goleta Murders," *Los
     Angeles Times*, July 29, 1981, https://www.newspapers.com/
     image/387467561/?terms=Cheri%2BDomingo.

57   Newspapers.com, "When Terror Reigned" *Sacramento Bee,* June 15, 1981,
     https://www.newspapers.com/image/621391759/]

58   Newspapers.com, "Frustrated by a Killer's Elusiveness," *Los Angeles Times*,
     May 27, 2018, https://www.newspapers.com/image/436953680/.

CHAPTER 11

59   Emily Shapiro, Whit Johnson, and Jenna Harrison, "'Golden State Killer'
     Suspect Threatened to Kill Family Dog, Yelled and Cursed in Neighborhood:
     Neighbors," *ABC News*, April 27, 2018, https://abcnews.go.com/US/golden-
     state-killer-suspect-threatened-kill-family-dog/story?id=54776065.

60   Official East Area Rapist/Golden State Killer, "The Voice of the East Area
     Rapist/Golden State Killer," October 23, 2017, video, 1:31, https://www.
     youtube.com/watch?v=Lc8xHJAeS7s.

CHAPTER 12

61   Redacted arrest warrant, Joseph James DeAngelo, 9.

62   Redacted arrest warrant, Joseph James DeAngelo, 52.

CHAPER 13

63 Julia Prodis Sulek, "'Golden State Killer': Neighbor of Suspect's Ex-Wife Said There 'Was Always Trouble,'" *Mercury News*, April 26, 2018, www.mercurynews.com/2018/04/26/golden-state-killer-neighbors-of-suspects-ex-wife-said-there-was-always-trouble/.

64 Sam Stanton, "Exclusive: Sacramento Cops Arrested Golden State Killer Suspect in 1996, Then Let Him Go," *Sacramento Bee*, March 15, 2019, https://www.sacbee.com/news/california/article227901874.html.

CHAPTER 14

65 Gina Pace, "'If He Did This, There Was Two Joes': Inside Golden State Killer Suspect Joseph DeAngelo's Quiet Suburban Life," *Oxygen*, August 5, 2018, https://www.oxygen.com/golden-state-killer-main-suspect/crime-time/inside-joseph-deangelo-suburban-life.

66 Ali Wolf, "Coworker, Friend Reveals New Details about East Area Rapist Suspect," *Fox40*, April 30, 2018, https://fox40.com/2018/04/30/coworker-friend-reveals-new-details-about-east-area-rapist-suspect/.

67 "Who Is He: The Life and History Joseph DeAngelo, the Alleged Golden State Killer," *ABC 7 News*, May 23, 2018, https://abc7news.com/who-is-he-the-life-and-history-of-the-alleged-golden-state-killer/3514158/.

68 Christine Pelisek, "Investigator Helped Catch the Golden State Killer—and He's Still Solving Crimes," *People*, June 7, 2019, https://people.com/crime/paul-holes-solving-crimes-golden-state/.

69 Redacted arrest warrant, Joseph James DeAngelo, 46.

70 Julia Prodis Sulek, "'I Hate You, Bonnie': Golden State Killer Likely Motivated by Animosity toward Ex-fiancée, Investigator Says," *Mercury News*, April 26, 2018, https://www.mercurynews.com/2018/04/26/i-hate-you-bonnie-golden-state-killer-likely-motivated-by-animosity-toward-ex-fiancee-investigator-says/.

71 Stephanie K. Baer, "Killer Witnessed Two Men Rape His Sister. It May Have Fueled His Rampage," updated May 14, 2018, *BuzzFeed News*, https://www.buzzfeednews.com/article/skbaer/the-suspected-golden-state-killer-witnessed-two-men-rape.

CHAPTER 16

72 US Department of Justice, *Serial Murder: Multi-Disciplinary Perspectives for Investigators*, Federal Bureau of Investigation, https://www.fbi.gov/stats-services/publications/serial-murder#two.

73 Radford/FGCU Serial Killer Research Database, Florida Gulf Coast University, https://www.fgcu.edu/skdb/.

74 Newspapers.com, "Murderer: Death Sentence Ruled for Bedroom Basher," *Los Angeles Times*, January 22, 1999, https://www.newspapers.com/image/160498275/?terms=Bedroom%2BBasher.

75 Larry Gerber, "Freed Man Believes Killer Deserves Fate," *Tulare Advance-Register*, January 22, 1999, https://www.newspapers.com/image/515461224/?terms=Bedroom%2BBasher.

76 Associated Press, "Death Penalty Upheld for 'Bedroom Basher' Killer of 6 in Orange County," *Orange County Register*, updated June 6, 2017, https://www.ocregister.com/2017/06/05/death-penalty-upheld-for-bedroom-basher-killer-of-six-in-orange-county/.

77 Janny Scott and John Dart, "Bundy's Tape Fuels Dispute on Porn, Antisocial Behavior." *Los Angeles Times,* January 30, 1989, https://www.newspapers.com/image/405210543/

78 Karen Hucks, "**Gary Ridgway's son holds memories of regular soccer dad,**" *The New Tribune, December 23, 2003,* https://www-1.thenewstribune.com/news/special-reports/article25855129.html#

79 William Lee, "End of Innocence," *Chicago Tribune* December 16, 2018, https://www.newspapers.com/image/513598057/

CHAPTER 17

80 Richard Winton and Matt Hamilton, "Juan Corona, Convicted in Slayings of 25 Farmworkers, Dies at 85," *Los Angeles Times*, March 4, 2019, https://www.latimes.com/local/lanow/la-me-juan-corona-serial-killer-dead-20190304-story.html.

81 Jack Welter, "Victims Buried in Orchards," *San Francisco Examiner*, May 26, 1971, https://www.newspapers.com/image/460428477/?terms=Juan%2BCorona.

82 Newspapers.com, "Evidence Against Corona Revealed," *Lompoc Record*, May 29, 1971, https://www.newspapers.com/image/540333509/?terms=Juan%2BCorona.

83 Benjamin H. Smith, "How Serial Killer Angel Resendiz Used Railroads to Target, Murder His 9 Victims," *Oxygen*, March 8, 2019, https://www.oxygen.com/mark-of-a-killer/crime-time/serial-killer-angel-resendiz-railroads-victims.

84 Paul de la Garza, "'Railroad Killer' Suspect Gives Up," *Chicago Tribune*, July 14, 1999, https://www.chicagotribune.com/news/ct-xpm-1999-07-14-9907140159-story.html.

85 Newspapers.com, "Accused Rail Killer Is Charged with Murder in Texas," *Intelligencer Journal*, July 15, 1999, https://www.newspapers.com/image/5667 74542/?terms=Rafael%2BResendez-Ramierez.

86 Mark Babineck, "FBI's Refusal to Share Credit for Capture Ruffles Feathers," *Monitor*, July 15, 1999, https://www.newspapers.com/image/331007919/?terms=Angel%2BMaturino%2BResendez.

87 Associated Press, "'Railroad Killer' Executed in Texas," *NBC News*, updated June 28, 2006, http://www.nbcnews.com/id/13579833/ns/us_news-crime_and_courts/t/railroad-killer-executed-texas/#.XWOCXuhKg2w.

88 Donna St. George, "The Country's First Known Female Serial Killer," *Asbury Park Press*, September 1, 1991, https://www.newspapers.com/image/145562053/?terms=Aileen%2BWuornos.

89 Associated Press, "Uncle Rebuts Wuornos' Tale of Abuse," *Florida Today*, January 30, 1992, https://www.newspapers.com/image/177202818/?terms=Aileen%2BWuornos.

CHAPTER 18

90 Radford/FGCU Serial Killer Research Database.

91 Zachary Crockett, "What Data on 3,000 Murderers and 10,000 Victims Tells Us about Serial Killers," *Vox*, December 2, 2016, https://www.vox.com/2016/12/2/13803158/serial-killers-victims-data.

92 Newspapers.com, "Frustrated by a Killer's Elusiveness."

93 David Taylor, "Are American Serial Killers a Dying Breed?," *The Guardian*, September 15, 2018, https://www.theguardian.com/us-news/2018/sep/15/are-american-serial-killers-a-dying-breed.

94   Scott Glover, "FBI Makes a Connection between Long-Haul Truckers, Serial Killings," *Los Angeles Times*, April 5, 2009, https://www.latimes.com/archives/la-xpm-2009-apr-05-me-serialkillers5-story.html.

95   Russell Working, "Arrest in Truck-Stop Death Shocks Farm Town," *Chicago Tribune*, July 18, 2007, https://www.chicagotribune.com/news/ct-xpm-2007-07-18-0707170835-story.html.

96   John Woolfolk, *The Mercury News*, "The 'Golden State Killer' Is Seen as a Relic As Serial Killings Fade in the Mass-Shooting Era," *Pittsburgh Post-Gazette*, April 30, 2018, https://www.post-gazette.com/news/nation/2018/04/30/The-Golden-State-Killer-is-seen-as-a-relic-as-serial-killings-fade-in-the-mass-shooting-era/stories/201804110333.

97   Crime Museum, https://www.crimemuseum.org/.

98   Anita Chabria, "Did the East Area Rapist Have an Accomplice? 'That Is a Possibility,' Detective Says," *Sacramento Bee*, May 7, 2018, https://www.sacbee.com/latest-news/article210658154.html.

CPSIA information can be obtained
at www.ICGtesting.com
Printed in the USA
LVHW012144010920
664769LV00012B/2350